Henry Charles Carey

Shall we have Peace? Peace Financial, and Peace Political?

Letters to the President Elect of the United States

Henry Charles Carey

Shall we have Peace? Peace Financial, and Peace Political?
Letters to the President Elect of the United States

ISBN/EAN: 9783744722087

Printed in Europe, USA, Canada, Australia, Japan

Cover: Foto ©Suzi / pixelio.de

More available books at **www.hansebooks.com**

SHALL WE HAVE PEACE?
PEACE FINANCIAL, AND PEACE POLITICAL?

LETTERS

TO THE

PRESIDENT ELECT OF THE UNITED STATES:

BY

H. C. CAREY.

PHILADELPHIA:
COLLINS, PRINTER. 705 JAYNE STREET.
1869.

SHALL WE HAVE PEACE?

Dear Sir:—

Let us have peace! In these brief words you express the unanimous wish of the loyal portion of the nation, North and South, and of whatsoever shade of color. It is the one great and preponderant desire of all that portion of our population which, at the close of a tedious and destructive war, has now succeeded in placing in the presidential chair the man to whom they had been most of all indebted for suppression of the armed rebellion. That there should be peace, and that it should be permanent, is to the true interest of all, whether loyalists or rebels, and it is in the interest of all that I now propound the great question, *Shall we have peace* —not a temporary one to be maintained by aid of military force, but such a peace as shall tend, day by day and year by year, so to bind together and consolidate the different portions of the Union as to render absolutely impossible a recurrence of scenes of war and waste like to those through which we so recently have passed? *Can* we have such a peace? For answer to this I have to say that such an one has recently, and on the largest scale, been established in Central Europe, and that all now needed among ourselves is that we study carefully what has there been done, and then imitate the great example which has there been set us.

Five and thirty years since, Germany presented to view a collection of loose fragments, most of which were mere tools in the hands of neighboring powers, France or England at one hour, Russia or Austria at another. A state of civil war had for centuries been the chronic condition of the country, and, as a necessary consequence, poverty, and such poverty as in our loyal States is entirely unknown, had, with but few exceptions, been the condition of all classes of her people.

Brief as is the period which has since elapsed, an empire has been there created embracing a population little short of 40,000,000, among whom education is universal; with a system of communications that, with the exception of those provided for the very dense populations and limited territories of England and Belgium, is not excelled by that of any other country; with an internal commerce as perfectly organized as any in the world, and growing from day to day with extraordinary rapidity; with a market on the land for nearly all its products, and, as a necessary consequence, with an agricultural population that grows daily in both intelligence and power; with a mercantile marine that now numbers more than 10,000 vessels; with a public treasury so well provided that not only has it made the recent war without need for negotiating loans, but that it has at once made large additions to the provision for

1

public education; and with private treasuries so well supplied as to enable its people not only with their own means to build their own furnaces and factories and construct their own roads, but also to furnish hundreds of millions to the improvident people of America, to be by them applied to the making of roads in a country the abundance of whose natural resources should long since have placed it in the position of money lender, rather than that now occupied of general money borrower.

To what now, has this all been due? To the quiet and simple operation of the protective features of the system of the Zoll-Verein, the most important measure of the century, and among the most important ever adopted in Europe. Under it labor has been everywhere economized. Under it, the producers and consumers of a whole nation have been brought into communication with each other, and thus has been created a great society which is destined ultimately, in all probability, to produce effects throughout the Eastern continent fully equal to any that may, by even the most sanguine, be hoped for in this Western one.

§ 2. Five and thirty years since, Germany and the American Union exhibited states of things directly antagonistic, the one to the other. The first was divided and disturbed, its internal commerce in every way embarrassed, its people and its various governments very poor, and with little hope in the future except that which resulted from the fact that negotiations were then on foot for the formation of a Customs Union, which, shortly after, was accomplished. In the other, on the contrary, everything was different, the internal commerce having been more active than had ever before been known, the public treasury filled to overflowing, the national debt on the eve of extinction, and capital so much abounding as to make demand, for the opening of mines, the building of houses and mills, and the construction of roads, for all the labor power of a people that then numbered thirteen millions.

The cause of these remarkable differences was to be found in the facts, that, up to that time, Germany had wholly failed to adopt such· measures of co-ordination as were needed for establishing circulation among its 30,000,000 of population; whereas, our Union had, five years before, and for the first time, adopted measures having for their object development of all the powers, physical, mental, or moral, of its people, all the wealth of its soil, and all the wonderful mineral deposits by which that soil was known to be underlaid. The one had failed to bring together the producer and consumer of food and wool, and had remained dependent upon traders in distant markets. The other had just then willed that such dependence should, at no distant time, come to an end; that producers and consumers should be brought together; and there had thence already resulted an activity of circulation and an improvement in physical and moral condition, the like of which had never before been known to be accomplished in so brief a period.

But little later (1835), the two countries are once again found totally opposed, Germany having adopted the American system and thus provided for freedom of internal commerce, America simultaneously adopting that which to Germany had proved so utterly disastrous, and which had been there rejected. Thenceforth the former moved steadily forward in the direction of creating a great domestic commerce, doing this by means of a railroad system which should so bind together her whole people as to forbid the idea of future separation. The result already exhibits itself in the quiet creation of the most powerful empire of Europe. The latter meanwhile has constructed great roads by means of which it has exported its soil, in the forms of tobacco, corn, and cotton, to distant markets, and has thus diminished its power to maintain internal commerce—the result obtained exhibiting itself in a great rebellion that has cost the country, North and South, half a million of lives, the crippling of hundreds of thousands of men, and an expenditure of more thousands of millions than, properly applied, would have doubled the incomes of its whole people, while making such demand for human force, mental, moral, and physical, as would, in a brief period, have secured the establishment of universal freedom, with benefit to all, white and black, landowner and laborer. Such have been the widely different results of two systems of public policy, the one of which looks to introducing into society that proper, orderly arrangement which is found in every well conducted private establishment, and by means of which each and every person employed is enabled to find the place for which nature had intended him ; the other, meanwhile, in accordance with the doctrine of *laisser faire*, requiring that government should abdicate the performance of its proper duties, wholly overlooking the fact that all the communities by which such teachings are carried into practical effect now exhibit themselves before the world in a state of utter ruin.

§ 3. Studying now our American railroad system, we find the great trunk lines to be, so far as regards the North and the South, purely sectional, all of them running east and west and the whole constituting a collection of spokes in a great wheel whose hub, wholly controlled by men like Laird and other workers in aid of the great rebellion, is found in Liverpool. As a consequence of this it had been that our dependence on such men had become more complete as those great lines had increased in number, and with every such increase our financial crises had become more frequent and more severe. Prior to the war a single turn of the British screw had sufficed for ruining thousands of those who had invested their means in the opening of mines, the building of furnaces or factories, and for thus crushing out the most important portions of our domestic commerce. With each such crisis there came increased necessity for scattering our people over the land, and for limiting ourselves to that single species of employment which is the essential characteristic of semi-barbarism—the raising of raw produce for the supply of distant markets. From year to year the tide of white emigration rose, following always the lines of road and canal of the extreme North, and carefully avoiding the Central States. Simultaneously, south of Mason and Dixon's line, a black emigration depleted the Centre, Virginia and Kentucky, Maryland and Delaware, furnishing the bone and the muscle required for consumption in the fields of Mississippi and of Texas. As a consequence of this, the extreme public education; and with private treasuries so well supplied as to enable its people not only with their own means to build their own furnaces and factories and construct their own roads, but also to furnish hundreds of millions to the improvident people of America, to be by them applied to the making of roads in a country the abundance of whose natural resources should long since have placed it in the position of money lender, rather than that now occupied of general money borrower.

To what now, has this all been due? To the quiet and simple operation of the protective features of the system of the Zoll-Verein, the most important measure of the century, and among the most important ever adopted in Europe. Under it labor has been everywhere economized. Under it, the producers and consumers of a whole nation have been brought into communication with each other, and thus has been created a great society which is destined ultimately, in all probability, to produce effects throughout the Eastern continent fully equal to any that may, by even the most sanguine, be hoped for in this Western one.

§ 2. Five and thirty years since, Germany and the American Union exhibited states of things directly antagonistic, the one to the other. The first was divided and disturbed, its internal commerce in every way embarrassed, its people and its various governments very poor, and with little hope in the future except that which resulted from the fact that negotiations were then on foot for the formation of a Customs Union, which, shortly after, was accomplished. In the other, on the contrary, everything was different, the internal commerce having been more active than had ever before been known, the public treasury filled to overflowing, the national debt on the eve of extinction, and capital so much abounding as to make demand, for the opening of mines, the building of houses and mills, and the construction of roads, for all the labor power of a people that then numbered thirteen millions.

The cause of these remarkable differences was to be found in the facts, that, up to that time, Germany had wholly failed to adopt such measures of co-ordination as were needed for establishing circulation among its 30,000,000 of population; whereas, our Union had, five years before, and for the first time, adopted measures having for their object development of all the powers, physical, mental, or moral, of its people, all the wealth of its soil, and all the wonderful mineral deposits by which that soil was known to be underlaid. The one had failed to bring together the producer and consumer of food and wool, and had remained dependent upon traders in distant markets. The other had just then willed that such dependence should, at no distant time, come to an end; that producers and consumers should be brought together; and there had thence already resulted an activity of circulation and an improvement in physical and moral condition, the like of which had never before been known to be accomplished in so brief a period.

But little later (1835), the two countries are once again found totally opposed, Germany having adopted the American system and thus provided for freedom of internal commerce, America simultaneously adopting that which to Germany had proved so utterly disastrous, and which had been there rejected. Thenceforth the former moved steadily forward in the direction of creating a great domestic commerce, doing this by means of a railroad system which should so bind together her whole people as to forbid the idea of future separation. The result already exhibits itself in the quiet creation of the most powerful empire of Europe. The latter meanwhile has constructed great roads by means of which it has exported its soil, in the forms of tobacco, corn, and cotton, to distant markets, and has thus diminished its power to maintain internal commerce—the result obtained exhibiting itself in a great rebellion that has cost the country, North and South, half a million of lives, the crippling of hundreds of thousands of men, and an expenditure of more thousands of millions than, properly applied, would have doubled the incomes of its whole people, while making such demand for human force, mental, moral, and physical, as would, in a brief period, have secured the establishment of universal freedom, with benefit to all, white and black, landowner and laborer. Such have been the widely different results of two systems of public policy, the one of which looks to introducing into society that proper, orderly arrangement which is found in every well conducted private establishment, and by means of which each and every person employed is enabled to find the place for which nature had intended him ; the other, meanwhile, in accordance with the doctrine of *laisser faire*, requiring that government should abdicate the performance of its proper duties, wholly overlooking the fact that all the communities by which such teachings are carried into practical effect now exhibit themselves before the world in a state of utter ruin.

§ 3. Studying now our American railroad system, we find the great trunk lines to be, so far as regards the North and the South, purely sectional, all of them running east and west and the whole constituting a collection of spokes in a great wheel whose hub, wholly controlled by men like Laird and other workers in aid of the great rebellion, is found in Liverpool. As a consequence of this it had been that our dependence on such men had become more complete as those great lines had increased in number, and with every such increase our financial crises had become more frequent and more severe. Prior to the war a single turn of the British screw had sufficed for ruining thousands of those who had invested their means in the opening of mines, the building of furnaces or factories, and for thus crushing out the most important portions of our domestic commerce. With each such crisis there came increased necessity for scattering our people over the land, and for limiting ourselves to that single species of employment which is the essential characteristic of semi-barbarism—the raising of raw produce for the supply of distant markets. From year to year the tide of white emigration rose, following always the lines of road and canal of the extreme North, and carefully avoiding the Central States. Simultaneously, south of Mason and Dixon's line, a black emigration depleted the Centre, Virginia and Kentucky, Maryland and Delaware, furnishing the bone and the muscle required for consumption in the fields of Mississippi and of Texas. As a consequence of this, the extreme mines, in building furnaces or factories, by means of which the consumers and producers of the South might be brought together. Can they have such aid? Apparently they cannot, millions upon millions being lavished upon Eastern and Western roads which, useful as they may eventually prove to be, tend now to intensification rather than to obliteration of the sectional feelings under which we have already so greatly suffered. Such roads need comparatively little help from government, Eastern capitalists being always ready for any measures tending to bring trade to the great cities, European or American, of the Atlantic coast. Northern and Southern roads—roads tending toward development of the extraordinary mineral wealth of the Central States—roads tending to enable the cotton of the South to reach mills and factories in the West—*do* need it, and for the reason that those capitalists are not yet so far enlightened as at all to appreciate the idea that the larger the domestic commerce the greater must be the power to purchase those finer commodities for which the Centre, the West, and the South are accustomed to look to Philadelphia and Baltimore, New York and Boston.

An expenditure for such purposes, involving an annual demand upon the Treasury for less than half a dozen millions, would add five times that amount to the annual public revenue, while giving to the domestic commerce a development that would add countless millions to the money value of labor and land, and by promoting immigration from abroad would do more for elevation of the down-trodden people of the eastern continent than has been done by all its sovereigns from the days of Charlemagne.

That we may have permanent peace, and that the desire of all loyal men may thus be realized, it is needed that our people be brought to understand that between the various portions of the Union there is a perfect harmony of real and permanent interests, all profiting by measures looking to establishment of perfect political and industrial independence, and all suffering from those which tend to prolong a dependence upon those foreign communities that hailed with so much joy the action of the men who initiated the great rebellion.

Throughout the world the tendency towards peace, freedom, and independence has grown as consumers and producers have been brought more nearly together, as the societary circulation has become more rapid, and as land and labor have become more productive. That peace may be here maintained—that all may really enjoy equality of rights—that the Union may be perpetuated—and, that the country may enjoy a real independence—we *must* have a system that shall tend towards enabling our whole people to make their exchanges with each other freed from the interference of foreign ships, or foreign merchants.

In another letter I propose to show the bearing of the measures above proposed upon the condition of the recently enfranchised people of the south, and through them on the Union at large, meanwhile remaining, with great regard and respect,

Yours, truly,

Gen. U. S. Grant.   HENRY C. CAREY.

Philadelphia, November 5, 1868.

LETTER SECOND.

DEAR SIR:

Little more than sixty years since the German people were in a condition so nearly akin to slavery that the chief difference between them and the colored people of our Southern States consisted in the fact, that while these latter could, the former could not, be sold at the horse block like other chattels. On the other hand, while the American slave had a positive money value that made it desirable to grant protection to children in their infancy, and to men and women in their age, the Germans had no such value except when, as with the Hessian sovereign of our Revolution, their masters could find opportunities for selling them by regiments as food for powder. Badly fed, badly clothed, wretchedly poor, and with no poor-laws by aid of which they might be enabled to demand assistance in case of illness, few, very few indeed, could command even the trifling means required for enabling them to seek abroad the subsistence denied to their families and themselves at home. Some few did then occasionally cross the Atlantic, but most generally as "redemptioners," liable to sale in open market for as many years of service as were then required for payment of their passages.

Such was the state of things throughout Germany when the disastrous campaign of Jena (1806), closely succeeding that of Ulm (1805), followed as it was by the almost entire subjugation by France of the German people, first awakened Prussian statesmen to an appreciation of the fact that if Prussia would ever resume her place in the family of nations she must look to the elevation of her whole people, and bring to a close her dependence on an effete landed aristocracy whose utter worthlessness had so recently been entirely proved. Prompt and energetic, the great man (Baron Stein) who then stood in the lead of Prussia, found himself before the close of another year prepared to announce arrangements by means of which the land was to become divided between those who theretofore had held it as property, and those by whom it had been cultivated, these latter passing at once from the condition of mere tenants at will to that of free proprietors. Thenceforth the Prussian peasant stood before the world as a freeman, and the effect of this was fully shown when, but a few years later, the Sovereign found it necessary to call to his aid the whole body of his people for expulsion of the French, and for liberation of that which then had become for them really a Fatherland.

The years which followed that expulsion were, however, years of British free trade, sad and sorrowful years, in the course of which there was little demand for German labor except so far as it was needed for that work of barbarism, the raising of raw produce for consumption in distant markets; years in which wool, rags, and wheat went abroad to be exchanged for other wool, rags, and wheat, converted by foreign labor into cloth, paper, and iron; years in which there was furnished daily evidence that poverty of the people and weakness of the government grew with every increase of distance between the producers and consumers of a nation. Nominally, the Prussian people had become free, but practically they were so entirely under the control of foreign traders that they profited little of that freedom.

Sad experience having soon and thoroughly satisfied Prussian statesmen of the absolute necessity for bringing consumers to the side of producers, and thus relieving farmers from the burdensome and oppressive tax of transportation, the year 1818 witnessed the establishment of a tariff that was thoroughly protective, and that looked to the establishment of a great domestic commerce. Not content, however, with the slight step which had thus·been made, they in the years that followed ·spared no efforts for bringing about an union of the various States of Germany on the footing of an entire freedom of internal intercourse similar to that which had so long existed in our American Union. Fiercely opposed in this by British agents, public and private, no less than seventeen years were required for its accomplishment; but the year 1835 at length witnessed the formation of that complete Customs Union which still exists, and to which the world at large stands indebted for the creation of a great empire which now stands first in Europe for the development, moral and material, of its people, and for the influence it exercises over the movements of the Eastern Continent.

Stein gave to the Prussian people that freedom which has everywhere been seen to result from division of the land, but to make it permanent, to extend it throughout Germany, and to prevent the retrograde movement which must inevitably have resulted from persistence in a policy which separated producers from consumers, and which looked to constant exportation of the soil in the form of rude products, it was needed that another great man, List, should make his appearance on the stage. At the cost of both property and life he did the work, and if we now seek his monument, we shall find it in the remarkable empire that has so recently appeared upon the European stage, described in my former letter.

Following the example set by Prussia, Russia, by dividing her land among those who previously had owned or cultivated it, has made one great step towards the establishment of freedom for her whole people. Thus far, however, the Emperor seems to have failed to see that there can be no real freedom for men who are compelled to waste their labor and to exhaust their soil by sending its products in their rudest forms to foreign markets. The day must, however, come when his eyes will be open to that great fact, and then, but not till then, will it be that the benevolent desires of those who had labored in the cause of Russian emancipation will stand a chance of being fully realized.

2. Failing altogether to profit by the great examples that had thus been set us, we have proclaimed emancipation while leaving all the l .nd in possession of its opponents; and have given the right of

suffrage to men who, as the recent election has proved to be the case, must exercise it in a way to please their late masters, or forfeit power to obtain bread for their wives and children. So far as regards public lands, the Homestead Law happily places all on an equal footing, but outside of this the union man, white or black, seems likely to enjoy no rights whatsoever.

As a slave the black man had a large money value, and it was greatly to the interest of planters to provide carefully for the women and the children, much of the year's profit arising from increase of *stock*. Now, having lost all such value, and having ceased to be mere chattels, the men are shot down by hundreds, while women and children perish for want of medical assistance. How small is the chance in this respect for black republicans may be seen from the following description of affairs as they exist in relation to whites in Edgecombe county, North Carolina, at the present moment:—

" Cases are frequently reported to me of physicians refusing to attend the sick, because their relatives were republicans, or expressed their intention to vote for Grant and Colfax. One man came into my office and told me that his little boy died on Monday for want of medical aid. No physician in the part of the country where he lived would attend the boy, because he was a radical ; one storekeeper kept him from eight o'clock in the morning until two o'clock in the afternoon, and would not sell him anything, because he persistently said he would vote for Grant. One man asked me to send for a northern physician, because the faculty of this country would not attend his wife, and she was at the point of death. Did I tell you about the affair in Wilson county a few weeks ago ? The authorities, all Rebels, and equal to Ku-Klux, arrested a colored man named Grimes, on the charge of burning a barn, but Grimes proved himself to any reasonable and unprejudiced mind *perfectly innocent*. But he is the leader of the Union League, and they wanted to rake him up, as he had made a severe speech against them and in favor of the radicals the day before. A delegation of colored men came for me twenty miles. I went. I asked for a hearing for Grimes in my presence. It was not granted. I offered to bail him. This offer was rejected. A Rebel drew his revolver on me in the court-house behind my back. Some one more prudent stopped his shooting. I left telling them I would have Grimes out, and the next morning they released him to prevent my having the gratification of doing it, so I was told. Grimes wouldn't promise them to vote for Seymour and Blair, but the next day he raised a company and went to the Raleigh Convention."

Nominally free, the condition of the blacks, in such a state of affairs, must be far worse than it had ever been before.

3. Nominally free, but really enslaved, the Irish people, long before the year (1846) of the great famine, were described by Thackeray as "starving by millions;" and by another high authority as having before them only the choice between "land at any rent on one hand, or starvation on the other." Famine and emigration having since largely reduced their number, and measures of confiscation having transferred a large portion of the soil from Irish to British hands, they now tell us of an increased prosperity of the Irish people; but on studying the real facts of the case we learn, that " at no period has their hold upon the land been so feeble and precarious as now;" that "the control of landlords over their tenants is practically absolute;" that "they can and do make by-laws on their estates which place the tenant for all practical purposes in a state of serfdom;" that "by those rules marriage has been known to be forbidden without license of the agent;" that "tenancy from year

to year is reduced by the contrivance of an annual notice to quit to actual tenancy at will;" and that "in some estates a receipt for rents is never given without a printed notice to quit on the back of it."*

The negro slave of our Southern States, more fortunate than the Irish one, had an actual money value, and of so great amount as to make it highly profitable for his owner to feed, clothe, and house him, to provide medical attendance, to care for his children, and generally to do nearly as well for him as he would for for his horses or his cattle. So absolutely valueless, on the contrary, has been the Irish slave that population has been declared to be "a nuisance," to be abated by means of any and every measure of oppression that could be devised; and when starvation had been followed by pestilence, this latter has been hailed as having, in the providence of God, been sent as a means of relieving the land from the burden of supporting so many useless mouths.

4. Such being Irish freedom, we may now advantageously study the condition of the agricultural population of England with a view to see what there has been and now is the effect of a monopoly of the land such as we have permitted to remain in our Southern States. Doing this, we find that whereas but recently we were told that it was to the south of England we were to look for the greatest agricultural degradation, when we turn our eyes to the Eastern counties we meet with the state of things here described:—

" 'The gang system,' as recently exhibited in Parliament, in brief is this: In the Fen districts, covering nearly a million of acres of the richest land in England, Huntingdonshire, Cambridgeshire, Nottinghamshire, Norfolk, Suffolk, and in parts of the counties of Northampton, Bedford, and Rutland, about seven thousand children, from five years of age and upwards, besides persons of both sexes of from fifteen to eighteen years of age—*are employed in gangs numbering from fifteen to twenty laborers in each gang, under a master, and in a condition differing from slavery only because it is infinitely worse.*

" The gang master is almost invariably a dissolute man, who cannot get steady employment as a laborer with any decent farmer. In most instances he actually purchases the labor of the children from poor parents; he sells this labor to farmers, pays the gang what he pleases, and puts the profit in his pocket. For seven or eight months in the year these gangs are driven, often seven or eight miles a day, to farms where they work at planting, weeding, picking, stone-gathering, and like labor, from half-past five in the morning to seven or eight o'clock in the evening. The gang-master is paid by the day or by the acre; and he pays the little children from fourpence to sixpence per day, while the older lads and girls receive from nine to fifteen pence. The master, for driving his hands to the field and for keeping them up to their work, which he does with a stick, makes an estimated profit of a pound sterling, or thereabouts, a week.

" There is testimony to show that hundreds of the younger children are carried home in the arms of the older lads every night. From working breast-high in wet grain many of the children are crippled for life by rheumatism, while others contract the seeds of ague, pleurisy, and consumption. Cases are given where little girls, four years old, have been driven through these long, terrible days of work. *The most pathetic pictures presented by Mr. Wilberforce of colonial slave-driving forty years ago, make the British West Indies seem almost an Arcadia in comparison with the Fen districts in England to-day.*

" This exhibition, shocking as it is, is by no means the most frightful phase of the gang system. The gangs are under no moral restraint whatever. Often-

---

* Morison. Irish Grievances shortly stated, pp. 33, 35. London, 1868.

times at night both sexes are huddled together in barns, where, among the older boys and girls, the most shameful events naturally follow. Clergymen and other respectable witnesses testified to the Commission of Inquiry that the gang laborers are 'beneath morals.' They have no consciousness of chastity, and do not know the meaning of the word. Medical directors of infirmaries state that gang girls, as young as thirteen years, have been brought to them to be confined. Their language and conduct are so depraved that dozens of parish clergymen, surgeons, and respectable laboring people, declared to the commission that the introduction of any gang labor in any village extinguishes morality."
—*Evening Post.*

Turning now to the west of England we find a state of things entirely in harmony with this, as may be seen by all of those who care to study the memoir of Canon Girdlestone, read before the British Association in August last.

The *Edinburgh Review*, just now published, questions the accuracy of some of the Canon's details, but admits that British agricultural laborers have before them no future but that of the slavery of the poor house—a slavery worse than that of our southern negroes in the past.

5. So long as the great Scottish proprietors could sell to the government the blood and bones of their subjects, creating regiments to be officered by sons and nephews, brothers and cousins of their own, everything was done to encourage increase of Highland population. That branch of the slave trade having, however, ceased to exist, and the slave having no longer a money value, people whose forefathers had for centuries occupied millions of acres have, by thousands and tens of thousands, been expelled from their little holdings, under circumstances of atrocity wholly without a parallel. The latest exhibit of these well-known atrocities, is given in the last (October) No. of the *Westminster Review*. The most prominent actors therein are found in the *liberal* families of Stafford and of Sutherland. Their most distinguished advocate is found in the *liberal* Duke of Argyle, so well known as author of the *Reign of Law*, which has passed through so many and so large editions.

6. The British and Irish people above referred to are really enslaved, although the law refuses to permit their being sold as chattels, and although the world is accustomed to speak of them as free. In what then does real freedom consist? Let us see!

Friday, on Crusoe's island, found no competition for the purchase of his services, and was, therefore, glad to sell himself on terms dictated by the man who could, if he would, both clothe and feed him, thus becoming the latter's slave. Had the island contained other Crusoes, their competition would have enabled him to make his selection among them all, exercising thus that power of self-government by which the freeman is distinguished from the wretched slaves above described.

Will you buy? Will you sell? The man who has a commodity, and must sell, is forced to ask the first of these questions; obtaining, for that reason, twenty or thirty per cent. less than what might be regarded as the fair market price. His neighbor, not forced to sell, waits for the second, thereby obtaining more, perhaps, than the ordinary price. Such being the case with commodities that can be kept on hand waiting for a purchaser, to how much greater extent must it not be so in reference to that labor power which results from the consumption of food, and which *cannot be held over for even a single instant.* The trader takes the market-price for his oranges, great as may be his loss; he stores his iron, waiting for a better market. The farmer sells his peaches on the instant, low as may be the price; but he holds his wheat and pota-toes, waiting for an advance. The laborer's commodity being yet more perishable than oranges or peaches, the necessity for its *instant* sale is still more urgent.

The farmer and the merchant having stored their sugar, or their wheat, can obtain advances, to be returned when their commodities are sold. The laborer can obtain no advance upon his present hour, his commodity perishing on the instant of production. It must be at once either sold or wasted.

Further, the merchant may continue to eat, drink, and wear clothing, his stock meanwhile perishing on his hands. The farmer may eat his potatoes, after failing to sell his peaches. The laborer must sell his potential energies, be they what they may, or perish for want of food. In regard to no commodity, therefore, is the effect resulting from the presence or absence of competition so great, as in relation to human force. Two men competing for its purchase, its owner becomes a freeman. Two others, competing for its sale, become enslaved. *The whole question of freedom or slavery for man is, therefore, embraced in that of competition."*

The more varied the employments, the greater is the tendency towards having the miner, the weaver, the spinner, the mason, and the carpenter, take their places by the side of the farmer; the greater becomes the competition for purchase of labor; the more does the land tend to become divided; the greater is the money value of labor and land; the more perfect is the farmer's in-dependence; the higher is the state of manners and morals; and the more perfect becomes the freedom of the whole people of whatsoever sex or age. In no part of the world is there at this moment so much competition as in New England for the *purchase* of labor, and in none, consequently, are its people so absolutely free. In none claiming in any manner to rank as civilized, has the contrary tendency so much existed as in Ireland. In none, therefore, has there been so universal a competition for the *sale* of labor; the consequences exhibiting themselves in the fact, that the occupant of land is now more than ever before a mere slave, holding his existence at the pleasure of the man who claims to own the land.

7. Thus far our measures of emancipation have resulted in giving to the negro slave just the same amount of freedom that has so long been enjoyed by the Irish slave, to wit, that he may, if he will, marry and beget children; that those children may not forcibly be taken from him; and that, although he may with impunity be shot or otherwise maltreated, he cannot be exchanged by his master against any given quantity of money. Wholly dependent for employment upon the men who own the land his situation is almost precisely that of the great mass of the Irish people, as here described by one of the most distinguished of English authors :—

13

"In a country in which every one who can find a landlord to accept him can be a farmer, and scarcely any one can be a laborer; where the three only alternatives are the occupation of land, beggary, or famine; where there is nothing to repress competition and everything to inflame it—the treaty between landlord and tenant is not a calm bargain, in which the tenant, having offered what he thinks the land worth to him, cares little whether his offer be accepted; it is a struggle like the struggle to buy bread in a besieged town, or to buy water in an African caravan. It is a struggle in which the landlord is tempted by an extravagant rent; the agent, by fees or by bribes; the person in possession, by a premium to take him to another country; and rivals are scared away by threats or punished by torture, mutilation, or murder. The successful competitor knows that he has engaged to pay a rent which will swallow the surplus, beyond the poorest maintenance for his family, that with his trifling stock he can force the land to produce. He knows that if he fails to pay he must expect ejectment, and that ejectment is beggary."—Senior. *Journals, Conversations, and Essays relating to Ireland, London,* 1868.

To four millions of people similarly situated we have given the right to vote in accordance with the orders of their masters, at the same time giving to those masters the right of representation in Congress for each and every one of them, thereby making a most important addition to the power that to the present time has been so much misused.

What is the use now to be made of the tremendous power thus accumulated in their hands is shown by the recent proceedings in Georgia and Louisiana. A year hence it will be the same elsewhere, and the day is not far distant when, if the national authorities do not interfere, the whole body of the States south of Mason and Dixon's line, with the possible exception of Tennessee, will be found engaged in a new, but peaceful, rebellion that must this time prove entirely successful, controlling Congress and placing in the presidential chair some man whose claim to that high office results from participation in the accursed rebellion so lately crushed.

Clearly seeing that such is likely to be the case, loyal Southern men are crying aloud for immigration, the rebel portion of the population meantime everywhere notifying Northern men that if they would save their lives they must flee the land, and thus preparing for a new rebellion in which they will be most heartily supported by all the rebel sympathizers of Northern States. Just now I have heard of the final expulsion, even from Eastern Tennessee, of a body of Scotchmen who had been sent there with a view to the introduction of the culture of long-wooled sheep.

8. The remedy for all this is to be found in creating competition with the landholders for purchase of negro labor, and thus giving to the slave that freedom which results from power to choose between employers in the field, in the mines, and in the workshop.

Why is it, however, that such competition had not long since existed? For the reason that our legislators have wholly failed to see that throughout the world freedom had come, *not as the result of mere proclamations,* but as a consequence of that diversification in the demand for human service which enables each and every individual to find the employment for which he had been intended, and for which he was most completely fitted. Look where they might they would have seen that slavery existed as a consequence of exclusive dependence on labors of the field. Correction of this, bringing with it freedom for all would have resulted from permanent maintenance of the protective tariff of 1842, as under it both the centre and the south would have been filled with furnaces and factories, thereby trebling the money value of land while greatly elevating the man who worked it. Great properties would gradually have become divided; the little proprietor—the man "whose touch," says Arthur Young, "turns sand into gold"—would long before this have made his appearance on the stage; the harmony of all real and permanent interests would have been hourly becoming more fully recognized; immigration would have attained proportions much greater than any it yet has seen; and the wealth and power of the Union would be thrice greater than now they are.

So rapid under the tariff of 1842 was the growth of Southern manufactures that in 1848 the editor of the *Charleston Mercury*, Mr. Barnwell Rhett, was led to predict that before the lapse of another decade the South would have ceased to export raw cotton. Unfortunately, however, for his prediction the South had just before placed the knife to its own throat by giving us the revenue tariff of 1846 in place of the protective one of 1842. From that hour Southern manufactures declined, with corresponding increase in the growth of that barbarous feeling which found its culmination in the atrocities of the late rebellion.

For the suppression of that rebellion we needed a million of men in arms. For prevention of the one that is now proposed, we need, and that at once, great armies of men and women carrying with them spades and ploughs, spindles and looms, sewing-machines and steam-engines, geographies and Testaments, and all other of the machinery by aid of which the people of the North have been becoming more prosperous and more free. For enabling such armies to move, and for giving them security while employed in carrying into full effect the great work of emancipation, we need that the government should, at the earliest moment, take measures for creating, and for placing in loyal hands, great lines of road by means of which the North and the South, the Northeast and the Southwest, the Northwest and the Southeast, should have between them communications as safe and rapid as those already existing between the shores of the Atlantic and the waters of the Mississippi.

To do this thoroughly and thus to bring the people now occupying the borders of the Hudson, the Delaware, and the Ohio, into direct and rapid communication with those of the Savannah and the Rio Grande, would involve an annual cost, as interest on the amount expended, less than would be required for maintenance of half a dozen regiments of men in arms; and yet, while preventing all future necessity for raising such regiments, it would so add to the productive power of the nation that the growth of wealth would soon be seen to be twice greater than at any former period.

With that growth would come division of the land, always a consequence of improvement in the means of communication and exchange. Freedmen, now wholly dependent upon planters for food and clothing, would find in road makers and furnace men competitors with their recent masters for purchase of their services, and would soon be seen accumulating little capitals by aid of which they might be enabled to enter upon and improve the little tracts secured to them by the Homestead Laws, and through many of which these roads would run. The already rich would be made richer by means of the increased value given to their properties, the now down-trodden negro race meanwhile becoming from hour to hour more free and independent. Harmony and peace would take the place of existing discord, and the various parts of the Union would become as thoroughly united as already are those of the great German Empire so recently created.

Let it now be understood that men and women who give themselves to the work of Southern development both can and will be sustained by all the powers of the government, and the negro will become really free, while the nation will become as really independent. Let this not be done, and the negro will be re-enslaved; the Union will be split up into fragments, as so recently has been the case with the great empire which now stands in the lead of Europe; and the men who have so nobly carried us through the late rebellion will have to regret that their labors have resulted in leaving the country in a condition far worse than that which had existed when Fort Sumter had been first assailed.

Earnestly hoping that a result very different from this may yet be reached, I remain,   Yours, very respectfully and truly,

Gen. U. S. Grant.   HENRY C. CAREY.

Philadelphia, November 9th, 1868.

LETTER THIRD.

Dear Sir:—

An eminent foreigner, speaking of our countrymen, characterized them as " the people who soonest forget yesterday," and that nothing could be more accurate is shown by the facts which I propose now to give, as follows:—

The revenue tariff period which followed the close, in 1815, of the great European war, was one of great distress both private and public. Severe financial crises bankrupted banks, merchants, and manufacturers; greatly contracted the market for labor and all its products; so far diminished the money value of property as to place the debtor everywhere in the power of his creditor; caused the transfer of a very large portion of it under the sheriff's hammer; and so far impaired the power of the people to contribute to the revenue that, trivial as were the public expenditures of that period, loans were required for enabling the Treasury to meet the demands upon it. Under the protective tariff of 1828 all was changed, and with a rapidity so great that but few years of its action were required for bringing the country up to a state of prosperity the like of which had never before been known, here or elsewhere; for annihilating the public debt; and for causing our people wholly to forget the state of almost ruin from which they so recently had been redeemed.

Returning once again, as a consequence of this forgetfulness, to the revenue tariff system, the troubles and distresses of the previous period were reproduced, the whole eight years of its existence presenting a series of contractions and expansions, ending in a state of weakness so extreme that bankruptcy was almost universal ; that labor was everywhere seeking in vain for employment; that the public credit was so entirely destroyed that the closing year of that unfortunate period exhibited the disgraceful fact of Commissioners, appointed by the Treasury, wandering throughout Europe and knocking at the door of all its principal banking houses without obtaining the loan of even a single dollar. Public and private distress now compelling a return to the protective system we find almost at once a reproduction of the prosperous days of the period from 1829 to 1835, public and private credit having been restored, and the demand for labor and its products having become greater than at any former period.

Once again, however, do we find our people forgetting that to the protective system had been due the marvellous changes that were then being witnessed, and again returning to that revenue tariff system, to which they had been indebted for the scenes of ruin which had marked the periods from 1817 to 1828, and from 1835 to 1842. California gold now, however, came in aid of free trade theories, and for a brief period our people really believed that protection was a dead issue and could never be again revived. With 1854, however, that delusion passed away, the years that followed, like those of the previous revenue tariff periods, having been marked by enormous expansions and contractions, financial crises, private ruin, and such destruction of the national credit that with the close of Mr. Buchanan's administration we find the treasury unable to obtain the trivial amount which was then required, except on payment of most enormous rates of interest.

Once again do we find the country driven to protection, and the public credit by its means so well established as to enable the treasury with little difficulty to obtain the means of carrying on a war whose annual cost was more than the total public expenditures of half a century, including the war with Great Britain of 1812. Thrice thus, with the tariffs of 1828, 1842, and 1860, has protection redeemed the country from almost ruin. Thrice thus, under the revenue tariffs of 1817, 1835, and 1846, has it been sunk so low that none could be found "so poor as do it reverence." Such having been our experience through half a century it might have been supposed that the question would be regarded now as settled, yet do we find among us men in office and out of office, secretaries and senators, owners of ships and railroads, farmers and laborers, denouncing the system under which at every period of its existence, and most especially in that of the recent war, they had so largely prospered—thereby proving how accurate has been the description of them above referred to, as "the people who soonest forget yesterday."

Such being the case, it seems to me that it might be well to show what was the actual state of affairs throughout the country in the revenue tariff years immediately preceding the war, and thereby enable railroad owners to study what had been the effect upon their interests that had resulted from the cry of cheap iron; ship owners to see that the decay of their interests had been the necessary result of a system under which internal commerce had been destroyed; laborers to see why it had been that labor had then been so super-abundant and so badly paid; farmers to see why it had been that their farms had then been so deeply mortgaged; secretaries to see why it had been that the public credit had then been so nearly annihilated; and all to see why it had been that the pro-slavery power had so largely grown as to have warranted the south in venturing on the late rebellion. To that end, I shall now present two letters written in 1858, and addressed to our then president, Mr. Buchanan, respectfully asking you to remark the predictions that further continuance in the same direction must result in financial and political ruin, and in our being driven from the ocean, all of which we now see to have been so fully realized.*

"Civilized communities—those communities, Mr. President, which have obtained that freedom of domestic intercourse which, as you have seen, we so sorely need—follow the advice of Adam Smith, in exporting their wool, and their corn, in the form of cloth, at little cost for transportation. Thus, France, in 1856, exported silks and cloths, clothing, paper, and articles of furniture, to the extent of $300,000,000; and yet the total weight was short of FIFTY THOUSAND TONS—requiring for its transport but forty ships of moderate size, and the services of perhaps 2000 persons.

"Barbarous, and semi-barbarous countries, on the contrary, export their commodities in their rudest state, at heavy cost for transportation. India sends the constituents of cloth—cotton, rice, and indigo—to exchange, in distant markets, for the cloth itself. Brazil sends raw sugar across the ocean, to exchange for that which has been refined. We send wheat and Indian corn, pork and flour, cotton and rice, fish, lumber, and naval stores, to be exchanged for knives and forks, silks and cottons, paper and China-ware. The total value of these commodities exported in 1856—high as were then the prices—was only $230,000,000; and yet, the American and foreign ships engaged in the work of transport were of the capacity of SIX MILLIONS, EIGHT HUNDRED AND TWENTY-TWO THOUSAND TONS, —requiring for their management no less than 269,000 persons.†

"In the movement of all this property, Mr. President, there is great expense for transportation. Who pays it? Ask the farmer of Iowa, and he will tell you, that he sells for 15 cents—and that, too, payable in the most worthless kind of paper—a bushel of corn that, when received in Manchester, commands a dollar; and that he, in

* These letters form part of a series entitled "Letters to the President of the United States on the Foreign and Domestic Policy of the Union and its Effects as exhibited in the Condition of the People and the State." Phila., 1858.

† This is the total tonnage that arrived from foreign countries, in that year. A small portion was required for the exportation of manufactured commodities, but it was so small as scarcely to require notice.

this manner, gives to the support of railroads and canals, ships and sailors, brokers and traders, *no less than eighty-five per cent. of the intrinsic value of his products.* Ask him once again, and he will tell you that while his bushel of corn will command, in Manchester, 18 or 20 yards of cotton cloth, he is obliged to content himself with little more than a single yard—*eighty-five per cent. of the clothing power of his corn having been taken, on the road,* as his contribution towards the tax imposed upon the country, for the maintenance of the machinery of that "free trade" which, as you, Mr. President, have so clearly seen, is the sort of freedom we do *not*, at present, need.*

" The country that exports the commodity of smallest bulk, is almost wholly freed from the exhausting tax of transportation. At Havre—ships being little needed for the outward voyage, while ships abound—the outward freights must be always very low.

" The community that exports the commodities of greatest bulk, must pay nearly all the cost of transportation. A score of ships being required to carry from our ports the lumber, wheat, or naval stores, the tobacco, or the cotton, required to pay for a single cargo of cloth, the outward freights must always be at, or near, that point which is required to pay for *the double voyage ;* and every planter knows, to his cost, how much the price of his cotton is dependent upon the rate of freight.

" In the first of these, Mr. President, employments become from day to day more thoroughly diversified ; the various human faculties become more and more developed ; the power of combination tends steadily to increase ; agriculture becomes more and more a science ; the land becomes more productive ; the societary movement becomes more stable and regular ; and the power to purchase machinery of every kind, whether ships, mills, or the precious metals, tends steadily to augment.

" In the last, the reverse of this is found, the pursuits of men becoming less diversified ; the demand for human faculty becoming more and more limited to that for mere brute force, or for the craft by which the savage is so much distinguished ; the power of asso-' ciation tending to decline ; agriculture becoming less and less a science, and the land becoming more and more exhausted ; the societary movement acquiring, more and more, the fitfulness and irregularity of movement you have so well described as existing among ourselves ; and the power to obtain machinery of any kind tending steadily to diminish.

" The first of these, Mr. President, may be found in the countries of Central and Northern Europe—those which follow in the lead of Colbert and of France. All of these are gradually emancipating themselves from the most oppressive of all taxes, the tax of trans-portation. All of them, therefore, are moving in the direction of growing wealth and power, with correspondent advance in civiliza-tion and in freedom.

" The last may be found in Ireland, India, Jamaica, Portugal,

* "Thirty-one independent States enjoying a thousand advantages and carry ing on a mutual free trade with each other. *That* is the 'free trade' that we really want."—BUCHANAN.

Turkey, and these United States—the countries which follow in the lead of England. All of these, are becoming more and more subjected to the tax of transportation. All of them, therefore, are declining in wealth and power, in civilization, and in freedom.

" In the first, the land yields more and more with each successive year—with constant increase in the power of a bushel of wheat, or a pound of wool, to purchase money. In the last, the land yields less from year to year, with constant tendency to decline in the price of food and cotton. The first import the precious metals. The last, export them. The first, find daily increase of power to maintain a specie circulation, as the basis of the higher and better currency supplied by banks. The last, are gradually losing the power to command a circulation of any kind, and tending more and more towards that barbaric system of commerce which consists in exchanging labor against food, or wool and corn against cloth.

" We may be told, however, Mr. President, that in return for the eighty-five per cent. of his products that, as we see, is paid by the farmer of Iowa, and by the Texan planter, we are obtaining a magnificent system of railroads—that our mercantile marine is rapidly increasing—that, by its means, we are to secure the command of the commerce of the world, &c. &c. How far all this is so, we may now inquire. To me, it certainly appears, that if this be really the road to wealth and power it would be well to require the exportation of wheat instead of flour, paddy in place of rice, cotton in the seed, corn in the ear, and lumber in the shape of logs, rather than in that of furniture.

" Looking, first, to our internal commerce, we find a mass of roads, most of which have been constructed by help of bonds bearing interest at the rate of 6, 8, or 10 per cent.—bonds that have been disposed of, in the market, at 60, 70, or 80 per cent. of their nominal value, and could not now, probably, be re-sold at more than half the price at which they orginally had been bought. Half made, and little likely ever to be completed, these roads are worked at great expense, while requiring constant and great repairs. As a consequence of this it is, that the original proprietors have almost wholly disappeared, the stock being of little worth. The total amount applied to the creation of railroads having been about $1,000,000,000, and the average present money value scarcely exceeding 40, if even 30, per cent., it follows that $600,000,000 have been sunk, and with them all power to make new roads. Never, at any period of our history, have we been, in this respect, so utterly helpless as at present. Nevertheless, the policy of the central government looks steadily to the dispersion of our people, to the occupation of new territories, to the creation of new States, and to the production of a necessity for further roads. *That, Mr. President, is the road to physical and moral decline, and political death, as will soon be proved, unless we change our course.*

" The railroad interest being in a state of utter ruin, we may now turn to the shipping one, with a view to see how far we are likely, by its aid, to obtain that command of the commerce of the world so surely promised to us by the author of the tariff of '46.

Should that prove to be moving in the same direction, the fact will certainly afford new and stronger proof of the perfect accuracy of your own views, Mr. President, as to the sort of freedom we so much require.

"In a state of barbarism, person and property being insecure, the rate of insurance is high. Passing thence towards civilization, security increases, and the rate of insurance declines, as we see it to be so rapidly doing, in reference to fire, in all the advancing countries of Europe. Our course, in reference to shipping, being in the opposite direction—security diminishing, when it should increase—the rate of insurance steadily advances, as here is shown:—

Rates of Insurance upon American Ships.

	1846.	1858.
To Cuba	1¼ per cent.	1½ to 2 per cent.
"Liverpool	1¼ "	1½ to 2 "
"India and China . .	1¾ "	2½ "
To and from Liverpool, on packet-ships, annual rates . .	5 "	8 "

"To what causes, Mr. President, are we to attribute this extraordinary change? May it not be found in the fact, that the more we abandon domestic commerce, and the larger the amount of taxation imposed upon our farmers for the maintenance of transporters, the greater becomes the recklessness of those who gain their living out of that taxation? Look back to the last free trade period—that from 1837 to 1841—and you will find phenomena corresponding precisely with those which are now exhibited, although not so great in magnitude. At present, the utter recklessness—the total absence of conscientious feeling—here exhibited, is such as to astonish the thinking men of Europe. Railroad accidents have become so numerous as scarcely to attract even the momentary attention of the reader, and the loss of life becomes greater from year to year. Steamers are exposed to the storms of the lakes that are scarcely fit to navigate our rivers. Ships that are unfit for carrying insurable merchandise, are employed in the carriage of unfortunate passengers, they being the only commodity for whose safe delivery the ship-owner cannot be made responsible. Week after week the records of our own and foreign courts furnish new evidence of decline in the feeling of responsibility which, thirty years since, characterized the owners of American ships, and the men therein employed.

"Look where we may, Mr. President, on the sea or on the land, evidences of demoralization must meet our view. 'Stores and dwellings'—and here I give the words of a New York journal—'are constructed of such wretched materials as scarcely to be able to sustain their own weight, and with apologies for walls which tumble to the ground, after being exposed to a rain of a few hours' duration, or to a wind which possesses sufficient force to set the dust of the highways in motion. Entire blocks of edifices are put up, with the joists of all so connected with each other, as to form a complete train for the speedy communication of fire from one to another. Joists are built into flues, so that the ends are exposed to becoming first heated, and then ignited by a flying spark. Rows of dwellings and warehouses are frequently covered with a single roof, which has not, in its whole extent of combustible material, a parapet wall, or other contrivance, to prevent the spread of the flames in the event of a conflagration.'

" The feeling of responsibility, Mr. President, grows with the growth of real civilization. It declines with the growth of that mock civilization, but real barbarism, which has its origin in the growing necessity for ships, wagons, and other machinery of transportation. The policy of the central government tends steadily towards its augmentation, and hence it is that American shipping so steadily declines in character, and in the proportions which it bears to that of the foreigners with whom we are required to place ourselves in competition.

" Two years since, we were told, that our shipping already exceeded 5,000,000 tons; that we had become the great maritime power of the world; and, of course, that this great fact was to be received as evidence of growing wealth and power. Last year, however, exhibited it as standing at only 4,871,000 tons, and future years are likely to show a large decrease—ships having become most unprofitable. More than four-fifths of the products of Western farms and Southwestern plantations, are, as we have seen, taken for the support of railroads and ships; and yet, the roads are bankrupt, while the ships have done little more, for some years past, than ruin the men who owned them. Such being the case, it seems little likely, that it is by means of sailing ships we are to acquire that control of the commerce of the world, so confidently promised when, in 1846, we were led to abandon the policy which looked to the creation of a domestic commerce as the true foundation of a great foreign one. What are the prospects in regard to that higher description of navigation which invokes the aid of steam, will be shown in another letter."

That letter will be given in my next, and, meanwhile, I remain with great respect,

Yours very truly,

Gen. U. S. Grant.   HENRY C. CAREY.

Philadelphia, December 10, 1868.

LETTER FOURTH.

Dear Sir:—

Steam is rapidly superseding sails, and the day is fast approaching when the latter will almost entirely have disappeared from the ocean; yet are we at this moment nowhere in the race. The time has been when we built ships for carriage of the produce of other lands, but the day has now arrived when we are almost wholly dependent on British and German steamers for commerce with the world, and for carriage of our own. Why this is so can, I think, be readily understood by all who care to study the state of things that existed ten years since, the date at which the following letter —being the second of those referred to in my last—was addressed to President Buchanan :—

"Every improvement in the construction of a ship tends to lessen the proportion borne by her tonnage, to the weight of the commodities to be moved. Every improvement in the quality of the commodities moved, tends to augment the proportions borne by the money value transported, to the tonnage of the ships required for its transportion. Here, Mr. President, is a simple principle by aid of which we may, perhaps, be enabled to arrive at some conclusion in reference to the tendency of our present policy—progress towards civilization having, everywhere, manifested itself in a diminution in the proportions borne by the machinery of transportation, to the value of the things transported.

"In the first year which followed adoption of the Compromise revenue tariff, that of 1834-5, we sent abroad, cotton and tobacco, food and lumber, to the amount of $92,000,000; and in that year, the shipping, domestic and foreign, that cleared for foreign ports, amounted to 2,030,000 tons. Six years later, in 1840-41, when the strictly revenue provision of that tariff had but begun to operate, we exported, of the same rude products, $98,000,000—the quantity of shipping clearing from our ports having, in the same period, risen to 2,353,000 tons. Two years since, after ten years experience of the revenue tariffs of 1846 and 1857, the total value of those exports was $230,000,000, while the quantity of shipping leaving for foreign ports amounted to little less than seven millions of tons—the increase in the former, in twenty-years, having been but 150 per cént., while that of the latter had been but little short of 350 per cent.

"If there is, Mr. President, any single proposition in social science that cannot be disputed it is *that wealth, civilization, and power, increase in the ratio of the diminution of the machinery required for performing the work of transportation.* On the turnpike, a single horse performs the work that before had been done by two ; and, on the railroad, a single car transports as great a weight as, at first, had been done by hundreds of horses and men, carts and wagons. With every movement in that direction, land acquires money value, and man becomes more free. With each and every one in the opposite direction, the value of land declines, and man becomes more and more enslaved.

"The first and heaviest tax, Mr. President, to be paid by land and labor is that of transportation ; and it is the only one, to which the claims of the State itself are forced to yield precedence. Increasing in geometrical proportion as the distance from market increases arithmetically, therefore it is, that agreeably to tables recently published, corn that would produce at market $24.75 per ton, is worth nothing at a distance of only a hundred and sixty miles, when the communication is by means of the ordinary wagon road—the cost of transportation being equal to the selling price. By railroad, under ordinary circumstances, that cost is but $2.40—leaving to the farmer $22.35, as the amount of tax saved to him by the construction of the road; and if we now take the product of an acre of land as averaging but a ton, the saving is equal to interest, at 6 per cent., on $370 an acre. Assuming the product of an acre of wheat to be twenty bushels, the saving is equal to the interest on $200; but, if we take the more bulky products—hay, potatoes, and turnips, it will be found to amount to thrice that sum. Hence it is, that an acre of land, near London, sells for thousands of dollars, while one of equal quality may be purchased in Iowa, or Wisconsin, for little more than a single dollar. The owner of the first enjoys the vast advantage of the endless circulation of its products—taking from it several crops in the year and returning to it at once, a quantity of manure equal to all he had abstracted; and thus improving his land from year to year. He is *making* a machine; whereas, his western competitor, forced to lose the manure, is *destroying* one. Having no transportation to pay, the former can raise those things of which the earth yields largely—as potatoes, carrots, or turnips; or those whose delicate character forbids that they should be carried to distant markets; and thus does he obtain a large reward for that continuous application of his faculties, and of his land, which results from the power of combination with his fellow-men.

"In the case of the latter, all is widely different. Having heavy transportation to pay, he cannot raise potatoes, turnips, or hay, because of them the earth yields by tons; as a consequence of which, they would be almost, even when not wholly, absorbed on the road to market. He may raise wheat, of which the earth yields by bushels; or cotton, of which it yields by pounds; but if he raise even Indian corn, he must manufacture it into pork before the cost of transportation can be so far diminished as to enable him to obtain a proper reward for labor. Rotation of crops being therefore a thing unknown to him, there can be no continuity of action in either himself or his land. His corn occupies the latter but a part of the year, while the necessity for renovating the soil, by means of fallows, causes a large portion of his farm to remain altogether idle—although the cost of maintaining roads and fences is precisely the same as if every acre were fully occupied.

"His time, too, being required only for certain portions of the year, much of it is altogether lost, as is that of his wagon and horses, the consumption of which latter is just as great as if they were always at work. He and they are in the condition of steam-engines constantly fed with fuel, while the engineer as regularly wastes the steam that is produced, a proceeding involving heavy loss of capital. Further stoppages of employment, both for his land and for himself, resulting from changes in the weather, are consequent upon this limitation in the variety of things that may be cultivated. His crop, perhaps, requires rain that does not come, and his corn, or cotton, perishes of drought. Once grown, it requires light and heat, but in their place come clouds and rain; and it and he are nearly ruined. The farmer near London, or Paris, is in the condition of an underwriter who has a thousand risks, some of which are maturing every day; whereas, the distant one is in that of a man who has risked his whole fortune on a single ship. Having made the voyage she arrives at the entrance of her destined port, when striking on a rock, she is lost, and her owner is ruined. Precisely such is the condition of the farmer who, having all at risk on his single crop, sees it destroyed by blight, or mildew, almost at the moment when he had expected to make his harvest. With isolated men, all pursuits are extra-hazardous. As they are enabled to approach each other and combine their efforts, the risks diminish, until they almost altogether disappear. Combination of action thus makes of society a general insurance office by help of which, each and all of its members are enabled to secure themselves against almost every imaginable risk.

"Great, however, Mr. President, as are these differences, they sink almost into insignificance compared with that which exists in reference to maintenance of the powers of the land. The farmer distant from market is always selling the soil, which constitutes his capital; whereas, the one near London not only returns to his land the refuse of its products, but adds thereto the manure resulting from consumption of the vast amount of wheat brought from Russia and America—of cotton brought from Carolina and India—of sugar, coffee, rice, and other commodities yielded by the tropics — of lumber and of wool, the products of Canada and Australia—not only maintaining the powers of his land, but increasing them from year to year.

"The more perfect the power of combination, the greater is the yield of the land; the higher are the prices of the rude products of the soil; the smaller is the bulk of the commodities to be transported; and the larger are the proportions borne by their value to the machinery required for their transportation. That, Mr. President, is the road towards civilization; but it is, also, the very opposite of the road that we ourselves are travelling, *the quantity of machinery required for the work of transportation increasing with a rapidity far greater than that which marks the growth of money values.* This latter being the certain road towards barbarism, we need look but little further for the causes of the decline in morals, wealth, and power, now so rapidly in progress throughout the Union.

"Power to command the use of improved machinery grows with the growth in money value of the things requiring to be transported, the farmer, whose proximity to the mill enables him to send his grain to market in the form of flour being far more able to contribute to the improvement of roads, than his fellow-farmer who is forced to send it in that of wheat. It diminishes as the things to be transported decline in value, and hence the weakness of countries like Portugal, Turkey, and India, that are becoming more and more dependent on distant markets. It diminishes with us, *and hence it is that our dependence on foreign countries, even for efficient means of transportation, so rapidly increases.*

"More than twenty years have now elapsed since the arrival of the *Great Western* steamer, and the establishment of the fact that we might avail ourselves of the power of steam for passage of the broad Atlantic. For nearly all that time we have been struggling to obtain steam communication, by means of American ships, with

Europe, the government aiding in the effort to the extent of many millions. What, however, has been the result of all our efforts? Ship after ship has been lost, until confidence in American steamers has almost disappeared, and with it the lines of steamers. The Collins line, as it still is called, now dispatches a single ship per month, and that, too, chiefly owned in Europe. The Havre line dispatches a monthly ship. The Bremen line has wholly disappeared. Mr. Vanderbilt has yet three ships engaged in the European trade, but the recent accident to one of them can scarcely fail to be felt injuriously by all. annihilating the little confidence that previously had existed. *The day is fast approaching, Mr. President, when no single steamer carrying the American flag will float upon the ocean, except goverament ships, and the very few private ones engaged in the coasting trade, in which foreign competition is wholly interdicted.* Such being the facts, and such the prospects, is it probable that we shall long maintain that superiority on the ocean which so certainly existed at the time when the general government entered upon the career of centralization? It would seem not. Beaten in agriculture, and beaten in manufactures, we are likely to be even yet more thoroughly distanced in regard to ships; and for the reason that our policy tends steadily towards lessening the value of the commodities seeking to be transported.

"The French policy—looking, as it does, to the emancipation of land and labor from the tax of transportation—is directly the reverse of ours. We tax ourselves for maintenance of the millions of tons of shipping required for transport of merchandise to be given to France, in exchange for millions upon millions of tons of food and other commodities, so reduced in bulk that their weight, in tons, is counted by thousands. Freed by that reduction *from all the cost of transportation*, France is enabled to invoke the aid of steam, and to such extent, too, that the arrivals of her own steamers, in her own ports, amounted in 1856 to no less than 8000 tons per week, and more than four hundred thousand in the year.

"France, Mr. President, is carrying out your own most excellent views in regard to commercial policy—laying a broad foundation of domestic commerce, as a means of obtaining the largest power of intercourse with the outer world. We, on the contrary, are destroying the domestic commerce, in the vain hope of thereby building up a great foreign one. Why have we no steamers running to Rio, to Buenos Ayres, to Montevideo, to Valparaiso, to Lima, or Australia? Because we have little to sell, except those rude products which the people of Brazil or Chili cannot use, and do not need to buy. Before they can do so those commodities must pass through the looms of Manchester or Mulhausen, and hence it is that nearly all our intercourse with the world is burthened with costs of transportation so enormous that our farmers are generally poor, although themselves owners of the land. In search of trade we fit out expeditions against Japan, involve ourselves in disputes with Paraguay and Buenos Ayres, explore African and South American rivers, and maintain an enormous diplomatic establishment throughout this continent; and yet have scarcely anything to sell, except to the people of France and England.

"What we need, Mr. President, is that real free trade which consists in maintaining direct intercourse with the world at large; but that we cannot have so long as we shall continue to export our commodities in their rudest state. The farmer who has but one mill at which to grind his grain has no freedom of trade. The miller and the baker have it, they being free to sell to whom they please. Our farmers and planters have none of it, being compelled to send their products to the distant mills before they and their neighbors can make exchanges, even among themselves. They need, as you so well have seen, that real free trade which would enable the planter of Mississippi to exchange with the farmer of Illinois, receiving cloth, lead, and iron in exchange for sugar and cotton. *That*, as you so well have said, is the free trade we want. That we may have it, we must diversify the employments of our people; we must enable them to combine their efforts; we must *relieve our farmers from a tax of transportation greater than is required for maintaining, ten times over, all the armies of Europe;* we must enable ourselves to pay our debts to the land, and thus obtain a real agriculture, in place of the system of spoliation that now exists; we must establish a balance of trade in our favor, enabling us to retain the precious metals and to maintain the real specie currency that you so much desire to see established. Those things done, we shall be able to command the use of machinery of exchange of the highest order—fleets of steamers taking the place of sailing ships, and the use of money becoming obtainable without the payment of a higher interest than is paid in any other country of the world claiming to be held as civilized. Such, Mr. President, is the real road to wealth and power; but, as you have seen, all our movements are in the reverse direction."

Forty years since the now great Germanic Empire owned less than a thousand ships. Two years since the number had already more than tenfold increased, and the day seems near at hand when it will again be greatly increased by the inclusion of Holland within the limits of that wonderfully growing Empire. Occupying now the first place on the land of Europe, it is being rapidly prepared for occupying one almost as distinguished on the ocean; and for thus perfecting a change of position wholly without parallel in the annals of the world, to have been accomplished in so brief a period.

To what, then, has all this been due? To the simple fact that enlightened German men have looked to the creation of a great domestic commerce as foundation on which to build a great foreign one, exchanging with the world at large cloth and paper instead of, as formerly, sending wheat, rags, and wool to the limited market of England. Then, the whole cost of transportation was borne by poor and wretched German farmers. Now, it is borne by those American and Australian farmers to whom Germany sends cloth and paper to be exchanged for wool and cotton.

Germany can now have that real free trade which results from finishing commodities and sending them, so finished, to all the ports of the civilized and barbaric world. We, on the contrary, have had that British free trade which has required that our farmers and planters should make nearly all their exchanges with the outer world in the single and diminutive market of England. They have sought the establishment of industrial independence, while we have sought a perpetuation of that industrial dependence in the face of which there can be no freedom for either man or nation.

Let me now pray you, my dear sir, to study the Reports on Commerce and Navigation, and to mark the fact that, while cotton stands alone in quantity, oil stands almost alone in the fact that we send it abroad fit for use. Turn next to the oil column, and see that with regard to it, and it almost alone, we have that real free trade which results from power to make direct exchanges, sending it to every part of the civilized world. Turn next to the cotton column, and see that it gives us little or no commerce except with England, France, and Germany, a score or two of ships being fully able to transport all that goes to other countries.

Germany has been building a true pyramid, of which a real agriculture was to be the basis and a foreign trade the apex. We have been building an inverted one, subjecting our farmers and planters to a tax of transportation so oppressive that the top-heavy edifice at length toppled over and came near burying all under the ruins.

So long as we shall insist upon limiting ourselves to the export of raw produce—the proper work of a semi-barbarous population—our exchanges must continue to be mainly made with those European countries which have already possessed themselves of steam navigation; and so long must we continue in our present state of helpless dependence. Whenever we shall have determined to export cloth instead of cotton, iron in place of corn, and machinery in the place of tobacco; whenever we shall have made ourselves industrially independent; then, and not until then, shall we regain that place on the ocean which we had occupied in the days when the now powerful Germany was a collection of scraps and fragments of territory, controlled in turn by France and England, Austria, or Russia.

To the development of her internal resources was England indebted for that control of the ocean which warranted her in saying that "not a sail but by permission spreads." So long as she held it there was there but little peace. Desiring now to enable our people peacefully and freely to communicate with the whole outer world, we shall find that the road by which we are to move in that direction leads through the establishment of such perfect protection as will enable us fully to develop the wonderful mineral resources by which, more than by anything else, our Union is distinguished from all other countries of the world. How that protection is to affect our growth in numbers I propose to show in another letter, meanwhile remaining, very respectfully, yours,

HENRY C. CAREY.

GEN. U. S. GRANT.

PHILADELPHIA, Dec. 10, 1868.

LETTER FIFTH.

DEAR SIR:—

That peace may prevail throughout the States recently in rebellion, and that harmony may be established among the various portions of the Union, it is indispensable that throughout the South and Southwest employments be diversified; that the habit of association and combination for useful purposes be enabled to arise; that mines be opened and furnaces built; that the wonderful natural resources of the country lying between the Potomac and the Rio Grande be developed; that the market be brought home to the farmers and planters of that great region of country; that between the various portions of the Union there be provided means of cheap and rapid intercourse; and, finally, that we establish among ourselves that great internal commerce to which Germany, as has been shown, stands now indebted for the commanding position she so speedily, by aid of the protective policy, has taken among the nations of the world.

That to such development it is we are to look for peace is from hour to hour becoming more clearly obvious to the people of the Southern States, and hence it is that each successive day brings with it new evidence of their anxious desire for promotion of immigration. West and Northwest, however, we find competition therein with the South and Southwest, millions upon millions of acres, capable of contributing on the largest scale to the comfort and happiness of our people, lying there wholly idle, even in states that have already long been represented in the councils of the Union. To meet all these demands we need to import *that only commodity which Europe stands prepared to give to us without demanding gold in payment—those only machines that increase in number and power the more they are usefully employed*—MEN, WOMEN, AND CHILDREN. What, however, are the circumstances under which such machines, more valuable than any engines, are most led to find a market among us for their service? Let us see!

Prior to the establishment of the first really protective tariff, that of 1828, immigration had been altogether insignificant, that of the whole decade ending in 1829 having given us little more than 100,000 persons. So soon, however, as that tariff had commenced to take effect immigration began to rise, and so strong and rapid was its growth that four years later it had already reached the extraordinary figure of 65,000, that large number of persons having been attracted by the great demand for labor which protection had created. Protection having been then abandoned, we find immigration to have become unsteady and irregular, the mean number for the decade ending in 1844 having been but 70,000. No sooner, however, had the tariff of 1842 become fairly active than we find the effect of protection exhibiting itself in the rapid rise of immigration from 74,000 in 1844, to no less than 234,000 in 1847—thus furnishing proof conclusive of rapid increase in the demand for, and compensation of, all human service. Under the revenue tariff of 1840–41 two men had everywhere been seeking employment at the hands of one employer. Under that of 1842 all had changed, employers having everywere been compelled to seek for labor, and liberally to pay for the service needed to be rendered.

The discovery of California gold deposits furnished a new variety of employment with large, but temporary, increase in the power to pay for labor, and under that stimulus immigration continued to increase until, in 1854, it passed beyond 400,000. Thenceforward, however, under the unhappy influence of the revenue tariffs of 1846 and 1857, it rapidly declined until in 1860–61 it had fallen to 112,000, or little more than its amount twenty years before. British free trade now gave us rebellion with further decline of immigration, which stood in 1861–2 at less than 70,000. Secession, however, gave, and most happily gave, to the loyal States the power of self-protection, and now we find the effect of the protective tariff of 1861 in the following figures exhibiting the number of persons who in the succeeding years were hither led to seek a market for their labor, to wit:—

1862–3	139,170
1863–4	193,754
1864–5	180,679
1865–6	330,725
1866–7	311,994

Extraordinary as is the growth here exhibited, it is far from presenting the entire truth, the number of persons who have transferred themselves from the unprotected British colonies to our protected States having been so large that were it added to the figures shown above, the total for the last three years would probably exceed a million.

The production of that million of people had cost the States of Europe at least A THOUSAND MILLIONS OF DOLLARS, yet did they furnish them in free gift to our Union. Had they given as much in engines, or other machinery, it would have been regarded as a wonderful addition to the wealth of the country; and yet, engines wear out with use, whereas men and women double and quadruple themselves, the quantity of such machinery increasing more rapidly in almost the exact proportion in which their services are made available to the purposes of the nation.

2. By aid of the protective tariff of 1842 immigration, as we see, more than trebled itself in the short period from 1844 to 1847, having been carried up from 74,000 to 234,000. Had that tariff been maintained, and had we continued to mine our own coal, smelt our own ores, and to make our own lead, copper, and iron, it would, with the aid of California gold discoveries, have been carried beyond half a million, and it would have since stood there, at the least, *giving with the natural increase a population ten millions greater than we have at present.* Forgetting, however, as they have always done, the troubles from which they had so recently been redeemed, our people had twice again repudiated

protection, and had thus reduced immigration, in the whole period of Mr. Buchanan's administration, to an average of 134,000, or little more than half a million in all. The revenue tariff policy of Mr. Walker and his friends then gave us a rebellion that has cost us, white and black, so great a destruction of life that more than all the immigration of Mr. Lincoln's period of presidential life was required to make amends for it.

Of all the legislative acts on record there is scarcely one that has worked an amount of injury so large as that which has resulted from the repeal of the tariff of 1842, forced upon the country by Mr. Walker and his friends. But for them our population would be now, at the least, one-fourth greater than it is at present, and our wealth more than twice as great! But for them, we should long since have achieved a perfect industrial, financial, and political independence! But for them iron would be so cheap that we should be consuming millions of tons, while exporting it to half the world!* But for them we should have had no civil war! But for them the slave would have been gradually becoming free, while his master would have been becoming rich! But for them harmony would now prevail throughout the Union, and the stars and stripes at this moment be floating over the largest mercantile marine the world had ever seen! But for them the demand on Europe for men, women, and children, to take part in the great work of developing our wonderful resources, would be now so great that capital would be everywhere seeking labor, while labor would be everywhere dictating to capital the terms on which it could be allowed to have its aid. That protection and freedom travel hand in hand together is proved by all the facts of our history, and the man who strikes at the former cannot claim to be otherwise than an enemy to the latter.

3. In accordance with the habit of the time, my dear sir, I have spoken of protective tariffs on one hand, and revenue tariffs on the other; and yet, when you shall have studied the facts which will now be given, you will, as I think, find yourself convinced that *the real revenue tariff is a protective one*, the free trade tariff, so called, being the one that so far depletes the treasury as naturally to bring about the state of weakness and of bankruptcy which now exists in each and all of the communities of the world that have found themselves unable or unwilling to defend themselves against the British free trade system.

In the four years by which the passage of the semi-protective tariff of 1824 had been preceded the customs revenue averaged but $16,000,000, and trivial as were the expenditures of that period, they so far exceeded the revenue as to make it necessary to borrow $10,000,000 in 1824 and 1825. In the four years 1826–29, with only semi-protection, the customs revenue rose to $22,000,000, and the necessity for borrowing wholly passed away. Under the really protective tariff of 1828 it rose to $26,000,000, and the public debt was then extinguished. The revenue tariff, so called, of 1840–42

---

* Of railroad iron alone our import in the present year will exceed 270,000 tons, and yet we have here such beds of coal and ore as are found in no other part of the civilized world.

gave but $15,000,000, and the treasury became literally bankrupt—money and credit having wholly disappeared. The protective tariff of 1842 gave $26,000,000 a year, and we found then no difficulty in raising all the money required for making the war with Mexico which terminated in the acquisition of California. Under the revenue tariff of 1857, with fifty per cent. more of population than had existed in the period of the tariff of 1842, we obtained but $47,000,-000, notwithstanding the wonderful addition to our resources resulting from discovery of California gold and Nevada silver.

Comparing now the protective tariff of 1828 with the revenue one of 1857, we find that notwithstanding the introduction of the railroad and the discovery of California treasures, the custom revenues had little more than doubled, while the population had more than a hundred and fifty per cent. increased. Comparing, again, the product of the free trade tariff of 1857 with the protective one of the last three years, we find that, although the population had grown but 25 per cent., the customs revenue had more than trebled. Such being the facts, the truth of the following propositions would seem to be now entirely established :—

First, That the more perfect the protection to domestic industry and the larger our strides toward industrial and political independence, the greater is the power of our people to contribute to the customs revenue:

Second, That the more domestic commerce is left unprotected, and the greater our industrial dependence, the smaller must be the customs revenue, and the greater the tendency toward bankruptcy of the people and the States.

Third, That the true road to freedom for man, to wealth, power and independence for the nation, lies through the pursuit of a policy which looks to the establishment of a great domestic commerce as the basis of a commerce with the outside world far greater than any we yet have known.

In face of all these facts, however, we are told, my dear sir, and by men claiming to be regarded as friends of freedom, that " from protection to serfdom there is but a single step, and that but one other is required to carry us on from serfdom to slavery. These three," as we are further assured, " are but links in the chain by means of which controlling spirits are enabled to confiscate, for their own proper benefit, the time, the forces, the labor, the capital, the liberty, and the rights of the great masses of their thus subjugated countrymen." Such being the views that, in a great variety of forms, are put forth daily by those who believe that, despite our recent unhappy experience, we should once again resume that course of action to which we stand indebted for all the losses of property and life inflicted by the late rebellion, it seems to me that it might be right and proper for you to ask of them to furnish answers to questions like the following, to wit :—

Why is it that, if protection be really adverse to freedom and to the general prosperity of our people, immigration always grows with such rapidity when protection is most complete ?

Why is it that, if British free trade is really favorable to freedom,

3

men who previously had come among us with intent to stay, have always then so largely re-emigrated to Europe?

Why it has been that in the last few years hundreds of thousands of Canadians have abandoned their free trade country, and have preferred to settle in these benighted and protected States?

Why it is that of the emigrants who arrive at Quebec and Montreal, and who have the choice between free trade on the one hand and protection on the other, nearly all prefer to take the latter, selecting homes in our Western States?

Why it is that Nova Scotia and New Brunswick are almost in a state of rebellion, because of their feeling of the absolute necessity for a closer connection with these protected States?

Why is it that nearly the whole population of Ireland would desire to fly from British freedom of trade and seek for homes in this now partially protected country?

Why is it that British emigration to Australia diminishes, and that to us increases, almost precisely as our protective policy is made more and more complete?*

Why is it that Australia, after a most severe political contest, has just now elected a protectionist parliament?

Why is it that when we build furnaces and open mines railroads are always profitable to their owners, and capital is easily obtained for the construction of new lines of road?

Why is it that when mines and furnaces are abandoned, railroad property so far declines that it becomes impossible to obtain the means for building further roads?

Why is it that financial crises, resulting in the ruin of trade, are the *never failing* accompaniments of the British free trade policy?

Why is it that such crises *never* occur in periods of protection?

Why is it that the deposits in our saving funds increase in times. of protection, and diminish in those of British free trade?

Why is it that sheriff's sales are so numerous in British free trade times, and so few in number in those of protection?

Why is it the revenue tariff periods always end in almost total failure of public revenues and almost total bankruptcy of the treasury?

Why is it that protective tariffs are so favorable to increase of public revenue, and to reduction of the public debt?

Why is it that a protective tariff now produces annually nearly as much revenue as was obtained by aid of a merely revenue one in the whole period of Mr. Buchanan's administration?

Why is it that the Republican party—the party of liberty, of

					To Australia.	To the United States.
*	1861	.	.	.	23,728	49,764
	1862	.	.	.	41,843†	58,706
	1863	.	.	.	53,054†	146,815
	1864	.	.	.	40,942†	147,042
	1865	.	.	.	37,282†	147,258
	1866	.	.	.	24,097	161,000
	1867	.	.	.	14,466	159,274

† In these years emigration was unnaturally stimulated by temporary increase of demand for Australian wool, consequent on failure in the supply of American cotton.

equal rights, of intelligence, and of sound morals—is so generally favorable to the protective policy?

Why is it that British free trade doctrines are so universally popular among men who believe in the divine origin of slavery—among sympathizers in the late rebellion—among foreign agents—among ignorant foreigners—and among the dangerous classes throughout the Union?

Why is it that, now that the South diversifies its industry by raising its own food, it obtains as much for 2,000,000 bales of cotton as before it had received for 4,000,000?

Why is it that when the refining of our oil, and fitting it for consumption, gives us now almost our only real free trade, the same results would not be obtained, and, on a much larger scale, by finishing our cotton and fitting it also for consumption?

Why is it that Belgium, the most prosperous little country in Europe, so earnestly adheres to protection?

Why is it that Russia, after a ten years' trial of British free trade, exhibits herself as a constant borrower throughout western Europe?

Why is it that Sweden is now in a state of so great suffering, after nearly a decade of British free trade?

Why is it that France, in making her last treaty with England, established a tariff more intelligently protective than our own?

Why is it that the maker of that treaty, Mons. Chevalier, had been led to tell his countrymen that—

" Every nation owes it to itself to seek the establishment of diversification in the pursuits of its people, as Germany and England have already done in regard to cottons and woollens, and as France herself has done in reference to so many and so widely-different kinds of manufacturing industry. Within these limits," as he further says, " it is not an abuse of power on the part of the Government; on the contrary, *it is the accomplishment of a positive duty so to act at each epoch in the progress of a nation, as to favor the taking possession of all the branches of industry whose acquisition is authorized by the nature of things.* Governments are, in effect, the personification of nations, and *it is required that they should exercise their influence in the direction indicated by the general interest, properly studied, and fully appreciated.*"

Why is it that Germany, the country that has most persistently carried into effect the policy thus recommended, now stands in the lead of Europe, although so recently a mere collection of loose fragments, ready to be moved about in whatsoever direction might be most agreeable to France or England at one moment, Russia or Austria at another?

Why is it that British policy, that policy whose imitation is urged upon us by all the advocates of that revenue tariff system which has so invariably resulted in destruction of the revenue, has so entirely crushed out of existence the whole race of those small British proprietors, " whose touch" according to Arthur Young, " turned sand into gold?"

Why is it that the British agricultural laborer has, by means of that policy, been reduced to a condition so nearly akin to slavery as to have before him no future but the poor house?

Why is it that all the countries of the earth which find themselves compelled to submit to the, so called, free trade policy now urged upon the world by British traders, are this day in little better than a state of ruin ?

You have said, my dear sir, Let us have peace ! Peace comes everywhere with general demand for labor; with good wages; with large demand for products of the farm, the furnace, the factory, and the plantation; and all these come with protection. Let us have protection, and let that protection be so definitively adopted as to give to all a perfect confidence in its continued maintenance, and all your wishes for the establishment and perpetuation of peace will be fully realized.

Greatly hoping that such may prove to be the case, I remain, very truly and respectfully, yours,   HENRY C. CAREY.

GEN. U. S. GRANT.

PHILADELPHIA, Dec. 17, 1868.

LETTER SIXTH.

DEAR SIR:—

More than anything else whatsoever the country needs financial peace. Shall we have it ? On the answer to this question depends, as I think, the decision as to whether or not the public faith is to be maintained—whether or not the Union is to be perpetuated.

Forgetful always, even of the events of yesterday, our people are particularly so in reference to financial questions, and therefore is it that we are now required to witness so many absurd attempts at bringing the country back, so far as regards machinery of circulation, to the point at which it had stood at the opening of the great rebellion. Scheme follows scheme, their authors wholly overlooking the facts, that the long period from 1815 to 1860, *with exception alone of the brief and happy periods of protection under the tariffs of* 1828 *and* 1842, had presented a constant series of financial crises, bringing ruin everywhere to unfortunate debtors, while enabling wealthy creditors largely to augment their already enormous fortunes; that in that period there had been no less than four general bank suspensions; that throughout the Centre and the West, the South and the Southwest, the average rate of interest had been higher than in any other country of the world, claiming to rank as civilized; that the money value of property everywhere had been almost wholly dependent on the condition of the English money market; that railroad proprietors, manufacturers, miners, and furnace men had, on repeated occasions, seen their property almost wholly swept away; that in each successive revenue tariff period a large portion of the lands and houses of the country had changed owners under the sheriff's hammer; and, finally, that rebellion was but the natural consequence of a system by means of which the Bank of England had been enabled, by a single turn of the screw, to withdraw from the country nearly the whole of the little specie basis on which our circulation has rested, thereby paralyzing the societary movement, and depriving both government and people of the means required for their support. What was the real state of things at the opening of the rebellion will now be shown, as follows :—

Had it been possible on the 4th of March, 1861, to take a bird's-eye view of the whole Union, the phenomena presenting themselves for examination would have been as follows :—

Millions of men and women would have been seen who were wholly or partially unemployed, because of inability to find persons able and willing to pay for service.

Hundreds of thousands of workmen, farmers, and shopkeepers would have been seen holding articles of various kinds for which no purchasers could be found.

Tens of thousands of country traders would have been seen poring over their books seeking, but vainly seeking, to discover in what direction they might look for obtaining the means with which to discharge their city debts.

Thousands of city traders would have been seen endeavoring to discover how they might obtain the means with which to pay their notes.

Thousands of mills, factories, furnaces, and workshops large and small, would have been seen standing idle while surrounded by persons who desired to be employed ; and

Tens of thousands of bank, factory, and railroad proprietors would have been seen despairing of obtaining dividends by means of which they might be enabled to go to market.

High above all these would have been seen a National Treasury wholly empty, and to all appearance little likely ever again to be filled.

Why was all this? The laborer needing food, and the farmer clothing, why did they not exchange? Because of the absence of power on the part of the former to give to the latter anything with which he could purchase either hats or coats.

The village shopkeeper desired to pay his city debts. Why did he not? Because the neighboring mill was standing idle, while men and women indebted to him were wholly unemployed.

The city trader could not meet his notes, because his village correspondents could not comply with their engagements. The doctor could not collect his bills. The landlord could not collect his rents ; and all, from laborer to landlord, found themselves compelled to refrain from the purchase of those commodities to whose consumption the National Treasury had been used to look for the supplies upon which it thus far had depended.

With all, the difficulty resulted from the one great fact already indicated in regard to the laborer. If *he* could have found any one willing to give him something that the farmer would accept from him in exchange for food—that the farmer could then pass to his neighbor shopkeeper in exchange for cloth—that that neighbor could then pass to the city trader in satisfaction of his debt—and that this latter could then pass to the bank, to his counsel, his physician, or his landlord—the *societary circulation* would at once have been re-established, and the public health restored.

That one thing, however, was scarcely anywhere to be found. Its

generic name was *money*, but the various species were known as
gold, silver, copper, and circulating notes. Some few persons possessed them in larger or smaller quantities; but, the total amount
being very small when compared with that which was required, their
owners would not part with the use of them except on terms so
onerous as to be ruinous to the borrowers. As a consequence of
this, the city trader paid ten, twelve, and fifteen per cent. per annum for the use of what he needed, charging twice that to the village shopkeeper, in the price of his goods. The latter, of course,
found it necessary to do the same by his neighbors, charging nearly
cent. per cent.; and thus was the whole burthen resulting from deficiency in the supply of a medium of exchange thrown upon the
class which least could bear it, the working people of the country—
farmers, mechanics, and laborers. As a consequence of this they
shrank in their proportions as the societary circulation became more
and more impeded, while with those who controlled the money
supply the effect exhibited itself in the erection of those great
palaces which now stand almost side by side with tenement houses,
whose occupants, men, women, and children, count by hundreds.
The rich thus grew richer as the poor grew poorer.

Why was all this? Why did they not use the gold of which
California had already sent us so many hundreds of millions? Because we had most carefully followed in the train of British free
trade teachers who had assured our people that the safe, true, and
certain road toward wealth and power was to be found in the direction of sending wheat, flour, corn, pork, and wool to England
in their rudest form, and then buying them back again, at quadruple
prices, paying the difference in the products of Californian mines!
Because we had in this manner, for a long period of years, been
selling whole skins for sixpence and buying back tails for a shill-
ing!* Because we had thus compelled our people to remain idle
while consuming food and clothing, the gold meanwhile being sent
to purchase other food and clothing for the workmen of London
and Paris, Lyons, Manchester, and Birmingham!

Why, however, when circulating notes could so easily be made,
did not the banks supply them, when all around them would so
gladly have allowed interest for their use? Because those notes
were redeemable in a commodity of which, although California
gave us much, we could no longer retain even the slightest portion,
the quantity required abroad for payment of heavy interest, and
for purchase of foreign food in the forms of cloth and iron,
having now become fully equal to the annual supply, and being at
times even in excess of it. That demand, too, was liable at any
moment to be increased by the sale in our market of certificates of
debt then held abroad to the extent of hundreds of millions, the
proceeds being claimed in gold, and thus causing ruin to the banks.
To be out of debt is to be out of danger, but to be in debt abroad
to the extent of hundreds of millions is to be always in danger of
both public and private bankruptcy. *The control of our whole*

---

* In the days of the Stuarts England exported raw materials and imported
finished products, and the people of the Rhine countries ridiculed them as fools
who sold whole skins for sixpences and bought back the tails for shillings.

domestic commerce was therefore entirely in the hands of foreigners who were from hour to hour becoming richer by means of compelling us to remain so dependent upon them that they could always fix the prices at which they would buy the skins, and those at which they would be willing to sell the tails. As a necessary consequence of this, the nation was not only paralyzed, but in danger of almost immediate death.

Such having been the state of things on the day of Mr. Lincoln's inauguration, let us now look at the remedy that was then required. Let us, for a moment, suppose the existence of an individual with wealth so great that all who knew him might have entire confidence in the performance of what he promised. Let us then suppose that he should have said to the laborers of the country, " Go into the mills, and I will see that your wages are paid ;" to the millers, " Employ these people, and I will see that your cloth is sold ;" to the farmers, " Give your food to the laborer and your wool to the millers, and I will see that your bills are at once discharged ;" to the shopkeepers, " Give your coffee and your sugar to the farmer, and I will see that payment shall forthwith be made ;" to the city traders, " Fill the orders of the village shopkeeper, and send your bills to me for payment ;" to the landlords, " Lease your houses and look to me for the rents ;" to all, " I have opened a *clearing house* for the whole country, and have done so with a view to enable every man to find on the instant a cash demand for his labor and its products, and my whole fortune has been pledged for the performance of my engagements ;" and then let us examine into the effects. At once the societary circulation would have been restored. Labor would have come into demand, thus doubling at once the productive power of the country. Food would have been demanded, and the farmer would have been enabled to improve his machinery of cultivation. Cloth would have been sold, and the spinner would have added to the number of his spindles. Coal and iron would have found increased demand, and mines and furnaces would have grown in numbers and in size. Houses becoming more productive, new ones would have been built. The *paralysis* would have passed away, life, activity, and energy having taken its place, all these wonderful effects having resulted from the simple pledge of one sufficient man that he would see the contracts carried out. He had pledged his credit and nothing more.

What is here supposed is almost precisely what was done by Mr. Lincoln and his administration, the only difference having been, that while in the one case the farmers and laborers had been required to report themselves to the single individual, the Government had, in the other, by actual purchase of labor and its products, and the grant of its pledges in a variety of shapes and forms, enabled each and every man in the country to arrange his business in the manner that to himself had seemed most advantageous. To the laborer it had said, We need your services, and in return will give you that which will enable your family to purchase food and clothing. To the farmer it had said, We need food, and will give you that by means of which you can pay the shopkeeper. To the manufacturer it had said, We need cloth, and will give you that which will enable you to settle with the workman and the farmer. To the naval constructor it had said, We need your ships, and will give you that which will enable you to purchase timber, iron, and engines. In this manner it was that domestic commerce has been stimulated into life, the result exhibiting itself in the facts, that while we increased to an extent never known before, the number of our houses and ships, our mills, mines, and furnaces, our supplies of food, cloth, and iron; and while we diversified our industry lo an extent that was absolutely marvellous; we were enabled to tend or pay to the Government thousands of millions of dollars, where before, under the system which made us wholly dependent on the mercy of the wealthy capitalists of England, it had been found difficult to furnish even tens of millions. The whole history of the world presents no case of a financial success so perfect.

In the physical body health is always the accompaniment of rapid circulation, disease that of a languid one. Now, for the first time since the settlement of these colonies, had our people had experience of the first. Every man who had desired to work, had found a purchaser for his labor. Every man who had had labor's products to sell, had found a ready market. Every man who had had a house to rent, had found a tenant. And why? Because the government had done for the whole nation what companies do for localities when they give them railroads in place of wagon roads. It had so facilitated exchange between consumers and producers, that both parties had been enabled to pay on the instant for all they had had need to purchase.

Important, however, as is all this, it is but a part of the great work that had been accomplished. With every stage of progress there had been a diminution in the general rate of interest, with constant tendency towards equality in the rate paid by farmers of the east and the west, by the owner of the little workshop and by him who owned the gigantic mill. For the first time in our history the real workingmen—the laborer, the mechanic, and the little village shopkeeper—had been enabled to command the use of the machinery of circulation at a moderate rate of interest. For the first time had nearly all been enabled to make their purchases cash in hand, and to select from among all the dealers those who would supply them cheapest. For the first time had this class known anything approaching to real independence; and therefore had it been that, notwithstanding the demands of the war, capital had so rapidly accumulated. The gain to the working people of the Union thus effected, had been more than the whole money cost of the war, and therefore they had cheerfully paid their taxes, while so many had been enabled to purchase the securities offered by the government.

Further than all this, we had for the first time acquired something approaching to a *national independence*. In all time past, the price of money having been wholly dependent on the price in England, the most important intelligence from beyond the Atlantic was that which was to be found in the price of British securities on the Exchange of London. With each arrival, therefore, our railroad shares went up or down because the Bank of England had seen fit to purchase a few Exchequer bills, or had found it necessary to part with some of those it previously had held. In all this there had been a change so complete that the price of British Consols had ceased entirely to enter into American calculations. The stride, in this respect alone, that had been made in the direction of independence, was worth to the country more than the whole money cost of the great war in which we are now engaged.

Throughout the war the government allied itself with the great body of the people, those who had money to borrow, interest to pay, labor and labors' products to sell, comprising nineteen-twentieths of our total population; and hence it was that the war resulted in success so entirely complete. Since then there has been a constant effort at separating the government from that great class, and bringing it into close alliance with that very trivial one, so far as numbers go, which profits by high rates of interest and low prices of labor and labors' products; and hence it is, that there has recently been so much danger of seeing control of the country pass into the hands of those who, North and South, had participated in the rebellion. To that end the greenback, *everywhere claimed as the people's money,* has by those in high places been denounced, small as is the quantity, when compared with the real need for it. To that end there has been an unremitted effort at leading farmers, laborers, and mechanics, to the belief that it had been a "forced loan," by means of which they had been daily robbed; that it had been, and still remains, "a dishonored and dishonorable currency," by the use of which they themselves were "becoming demoralized;" that as a consequence of its use they were "in danger of losing that sense of honor which is necessary for the well-being of society;" that to its continued use they had been indebted since the war for "instability of prices, unsteadiness in trade," and a variety of other ills, whose general effect is, as we are assured by no less an authority than that of our Finance Minister, that of "filling the coffers of the rich," while making the country absolutely "intolerable to persons of limited incomes."

The person to whom we are just now indebted for this last and worst description of the evils under which we labor, may, my dear sir, certainly be classed among those who most entirely discharge from their memories all recollection of yesterday's events. Had it been otherwise with him he would have seen that, with exception of the years of the protective tariffs of 1828 and 1842, the whole of the period from 1815 to 1860 had exhibited a succession of changes infinitely greater and more injurious to both people and government than any that had been known since the greenback had been issued; since the nation first assumed performance of the duty of furnishing a basis for our monetary transactions not liable to be withdrawn at any and every moment of change in the policy of the Bank of England, as had been the case in all those periods at which we had pretended to maintain the use of the precious metals, while pursuing a revenue tariff policy which compelled an export of the whole gold produce of California.

Less forgetful than the Secretary, those who have labor to sell and money to buy, the vast majority of our people, cling to the ex-

isting state of things, and anxiously desire to witness a restoration
of that financial peace which had prevailed at the moment when the
former, in his memorable Fort Wayne speech, fulminated his declaration of financial war. From that hour he has been in close
alliance with the money lending class, receivers of interest, and
livers on incomes, with them asserting that circulating notes were
greatly in excess of the public needs; that the national honor demanded a substitution of gold for notes; and that suppression of
the latter would be followed by such increased supplies of the former
as would at once fill the vacuum thus created; thereby doing
all in his power toward destroying that faith in the future to
which we had been indebted for success in war, and to which we
must be indebted for power to resume should resumption ever again
be brought about.

How absurd are such assertions, and how little they are calcu-
lated to bear examination, will, as I think, become obvious, my dear
sir, when you have reflected on the following facts:—

With a population scarcely larger than our own, grouped together on a surface less than that of half a dozen of our States and
therefore having far less need than ourselves of any material medium
of exchange, France has a circulating medium one-half greater than
is allowed to us.

With a still more compressed population, and one far more accustomed to effecting exchanges without the use of any species of
money whatsoever, Great Britain and Ireland use more than twenty
dollars per head.

With less than forty millions of people, scattered over almost a
continent, *and therefore standing thrice as much in need of some
material medium of circulation*, we are allowed far less than is
given in either France or Britain. When, however, we look to those
portions in which population is dense, and money by comparison
little needed, we find them using more than either France or England, the actual circulation of New England being more than thirty
dollars per head.

Looking next South and West, we find in many of the States and
territories hardly even a single one, and with scarcely the smallest
chance that more than one will ever be allowed them. To assert,
under such circumstances, that there is any excess of circulation, is
so utterly absurd as to make it almost doubtful if the gentleman
who writes treasury and currency reports, and those others who
make resumption speeches, can really believe the strange assertions
they have been used to make. To seek, by means of action in the
direction such men now indicate, a resumption of specie payments,
must result in failure so complete as to postpone any real resumption for half a century to come.

What the country really needs is an increase, and not a decrease,
in the machinery of circulation. That, however, as we are assured,
will readily be obtained if the circulating notes can only be sup-
pressed. Create a need for the precious metals, and they will be
sure to come. Why, however, is it, that it is precisely where circu-
latory notes most abound, in New England, Old England, France,
and Belgium, that gold and silver are most attracted? Why is it,

that in the almost total absence of circulating notes, the precious metals have so entirely disappeared from Georgia and Alabama, North and South Carolina? Why is it, pending the existence of the state of affairs here below described, the precious metals fly from *Utah* and its immediate neighborhood?

"You have tight money markets sometimes in the East. I have read of how semi-savage nations 'barter.' I saw it cited, as a curious fact, in the newspapers, that in Georgia eggs are used as small change; but in Utah I see around me a people, a prosperous people, doing the business of life almost without any money at all. In Salt Lake City itself, right in the line of travel, there is some money; but in the country settlements, which radiate thence into every valley and by every watercourse for a hundred miles, it is literally true that they have no circulating medium. Wheat is the usual legal tender of the country. Horses, harness, vehicles, cattle, and hay, are cash; eggs, butter, pistols, knives, stockings, and whisky, are change; pumpkins, potatoes, sorghum, molasses, and calves, are 'shinplasters,' which are taken at a discount, and with which the saints delight to pay their debts (if it is ever a delight to pay debts). Business in this community, with this currency, is a very curious and amusing pastime. A peddler, for instance, could take out his goods in a carpet-bag, but would need a 'bull' train to freight back his money. I knew a man who refused an offer to work in the country at fifty dollars a month because he would need a 'forty-hundred wagon and four yoke of oxen' to haul his week's wages to the whisky-shop, theatre, &c., on Saturday evening. When a man once lays out his money in any kind of property, it is next to impossible to reconvert it into money. There is many a man here, who, when he first came into the valley, had no intention of remaining but a short time, but soon got so involved that he could never get away without making heavy pecuniary sacrifices. Property is a Proteus, which you must continue to grip firmly, notwithstanding his slippery changes, until you have him in his true shape. Now you have him as a fine horse and saddle; presto, he is only sixty gallons of sorghum molasses; now he changes into two cows and a calf, and before you have time to think he is transformed into fifteen cords of wood up in the mountain canon; next he becomes a yoke of oxen; then a 'shutler' wagon; ha! is he about to slip from you at last in the form of bad debts?"

The following passage from a letter just received from Iowa, shows how completely the financial policy of our Financial Minister tends to place the many who have to borrow at the mercy of the few who are able to lend:—

"When the banks have money to loan it can be borrowed for 10 per cent. interest per annum; but sometimes, and very often, they are short and refuse to loan except to their daily customers. Then the occasional borrower is thrown upon the tender mercies of money men, many of whom indeed are bankers, and is forced to pay 30 and sometimes 40 per cent. This is, of course, done in an underhand way, so that the law cannot reach the extortioner, but it could not be done *at all* if we had circulation enough."

The picture here presented is that of the whole country south and west of Pennsylvania, yet are we daily treated with prescriptions for financial cure based upon the idea of making more and more scarce that machinery of circulation for use of which poor men are already paying 30 or 40 per cent. per annum!

Careful study of the facts here given might, perhaps, satisfy our Finance Minister, that the more thoroughly the channels of circulation are supplied with the cheaper commodity, as is now the case in all New England, *the greater is the power to purchase the precious metals and the less the need for them.* What is now most required is an increase of the former and a diminution of the latter, every step in that direction tending towards reduction of that premium on gold, of which complaint is made.

That such reduction may be brought about, there must be a restoration of that confidence which the Secretary has so studiously labored to destroy. Such restoration may be looked for when our reformers shall have determined to study a very little of that past, which they have so evidently forgotten. Studying it, they will be led to see that, with the single exception of the protective periods above referred to, at no time in our history has the price of gold, as measured in corn or cotton, cloth or houses, farms or furnaces, remained so steady as in the four years through which we have just now passed.

Within those years we have closed a war which was costing three millions a day, and have entered upon a state of peace the cost of which is less than half a million; and yet, sudden as was the change, the bankruptcies and sheriff's sales have not been a fifth as great in number as those produced in nominally specie-paying, and really British free-trade, times, in a single year. Never in the whole history of the world has so great a change been so little felt; and the reason why it has been so is, *that the substratum of our whole monetary system consisted of a commodity for which there was no demand in foreign markets.*

That we should at all times hold in mind that resumption must eventually be reached, is not at all to be questioned. That it may be so reached as to give us increased prosperity, it must be sought in a direction very different from any yet indicated by our many monetary reformers, whether editors, senators, or finance ministers.

What that direction is I propose to state in a future letter, and meanwhile remain, with great regard and respect, yours truly,

HENRY C. CAREY.

Philadelphia, December 21, 1868.

LETTER SEVENTH.

DEAR SIR :—

The cheapest, most effective, and most important of all the machinery by means of which property is enabled to pass from hand to hand, and thus to become *current*, is found in *the credit* and *the check* by whose aid thousands of millions pass in Wall Street with less use of any material medium of circulation than among the Rocky Mountains would be required for arrangement of transactions counting by hundreds, or by thousands.

Next to them comes *the circulating note*, the most generally useful, the most harmless, and the most calumniated of all the labor saving machinery ever invented by man.

Last of all—the most cumbrous, most expensive, and least effective of all the machinery of circulation in use among people claiming to be civilized—come the precious metals themselves, and for that reason, probably, the most admired by such financiers as our actual President and his Finance Minister, the two uniting in denouncing the circulating note as the inferior currency by means of which the superior one, consisting of the metals themselves, is, as they assure us, driven out of use.

When, however, the honorable Secretary comes to compare the working of *the credit* and *the note*, he assures us that so far is the inferior note from expelling the superior credit, that it is this latter which is continually thrusting the former out of use, in the manner that here is shown :—

" In all the cities and towns throughout the country checks upon credits in banks and bills of exchange have largely taken the place of bank notes. Not a fiftieth part of the business of the large cities is transacted by the actual use of money, and what is true in regard to the business of the chief of cities is measurably true in regard to that of towns and villages throughout the country. Everywhere bank credits and bills of exchange perform the office of currency to a much greater extent than in former years. Except in dealings with the government, for retail trade, for the payment of labor and taxes, for travelling expenses, the purchase of products at first hand, and for the bankers' reserve, money is hardly a necessity. The increased use of bank checks and bills of exchange counterbalances the increased demand for money resulting from the curtailment of mercantile credits."—*Report of the Secretary of the Treasury on the State of the Finances for the year* 1867.

This is all perfectly true. The superior currency of *the check* and *the credit* tends to lessen demand for the inferior *note*, just as the locomotive lessens demand for the wagon—the *note* in its turn displacing the precious metals just as the wagon displaces the mule and the pack-saddle. Any attempt, therefore, at driving *the note* from use, with a view to compel increased use of the metals, is as much in opposition to the progress of civilization as would be a law forbidding use of the telegraph with a view to compel increased use of the facilities of intercourse furnished by the post office and the railroad train.

The great labor-saving machine is *the credit*. The next is *the circulating note*. Last come *the metals*, by means of which men are enabled to pass from the slow and costly operation of barter to the more rapid one of purchase and sale. Why then do not all men prefer the cheap *credit* even to the slightly expensive *note ?* For the reason that credit itself can have no existence among a poor and widely scattered population. It abounds in England and New England, but has no existence in the regions of the Rocky Mountains and Rio Grande. Why, then, do these latter not even adopt *the note ?* For the reason that they are not yet so far advanced in civilization as to have among themselves either individuals or corporations capable of making notes such as would readily be received in exchange for property of any description whatsoever. *The need for such notes, proportioned to the exchanges required to be made, is a thousand times greater than it is in Wall Street ;* and it exists everywhere in the precise ratio of the absence of the check, the draft, the clearing house, and all other of the various contrivances for dispensing with the services of either the precious metals or the circulating note.

Between these two descriptions of superior currency there are these important differences, to wit:—

That *the note* represents actual property of the parties by whom it is issued, that property having been deposited in the Treasury as scurity for its redemption ; whereas *the credit* represents property temporarily deposited in the banks, and liable to be claimed at any instant :

That, while *the note* cannot be so used as in any manner to change its relation to the total currency, *the credit* may be, and habitually is, so used as to *duplicate* its relation thereto—A, the actual owner, and B, the temporary user thereof, both exercising equal power of purchase and equal power to create a currency of checks or drafts —that superior one with the growth of which there should be diminished need for circulating notes :

That, as the inferior of these two currencies—*the note*—yields no interest to its *holder*, all desire to circumscribe within the narrowest limits the quantity to be kept on hand :

That, as the superior one—*the credit*—yields interest to its *makers*, banks and bankers seek as far as possible to increase it by lending out all the moneys standing to the credit of their customers:

That, as the people at large find their interest promoted by limiting the use of *circulating notes* the quantity in actual use changes, under ordinary circumstances, so slowly as scarcely to be perceived; whereas, the quantity *of credits*, dependent as it is upon the arbitrary will of banks and bankers, changes from hour to hour, and with a rapidity that sets at defiance all calculation :

That, consequently, *it is the power to create the superior currency, that based on mere credits, which demands to be regulated by law ;* and *not* that inferior one which is based on property, and which finds its proper regulation in the need for its use by the masses of the people.

These things premised, we may now study the course of things under the State bank system, taking as its type the returns of 1860, as follows, the figures representing millions :—

	Capital.	Circulation.	Capital and circulation.	Investments.	Excess investm'ts.
Total amount	422	207	629	807	178
New York and New England	235	73	308	443	135
All other States and Territories	187	134	321	364	43

The first thing that strikes us on an examination of this table is the entire harmony of the facts here presented with the theory of the Secretary, and with the general impressions on the subject, the proportion of circulating notes to capital and business having been very small in those States in which a credit currency most abounded, and very large in those in which such credits were least abundant. With a bank capital of but $235,000,000, New York and New England had the use of $135,000,000 of credits created by banks for their own use and profit, being nearly twice more than the amount of their circulation. With a capital only one-fifth less, the remaining people of the Union appear to have enjoyed the advantages of the superior currency to the extent of but $43,000,000, and their banks to have been dependent upon the profits of circulation to an amount equal to three-fourths of their whole capital, being about twice that of the trading States above enumerated.

The total currency created by banks for their own profit appears to have been as follows :—

New York and New England, with a population of 7,000,000, and a wealth, as returned by the census, of $3,707,000,000, had credits based upon moneys temporarily in banks to the extent of $135,000,000
Circulation 73,000,000

Total $208,000,000

The remaining States, with a population exceeding twenty-four millions, and a wealth of $11,558,000,000, or more than thrice greater, had a bank-created currency thus composed, to wit :—

Credits $43,000,000
Circulation 134,000,000

$177,000,000

In the one case banks might have lived and prospered, even had they been wholly deprived of the profits of circulation. In the other, outside of a few cities, no bank deprived of those profits could have existed.

Fully enjoying the advantages of both the people of the one could generally have the use of money at about the legal rate of interest. Limited almost entirely to the circulation, and that itself in many cases limited by absurd restrictions, those of the other were accustomed to pay twice, thrice, and even four times that rate. With the one prompt payment was a thing of general occurrence. With the other, debt was almost universal, not because of want of property, but because throughout a large portion of the country there existed neither credits, circulating notes, nor any other general medium of exchange whatsoever.

Such having been the state of things seven years since, under the State bank system, we may now examine the working of the, so-styled, national system, with a view to see if it has tended to correction or to exaggeration of the difficulties that then existed.

§ 2. Under the State bank system, as has been shown, the distribution of *credits* and *circulation* among the States was very nearly in accordance with the Secretary's present teachings. How far it is so now, under this, so-called, national one, organized by the Secretary himself, it is proposed here to show.

By the report of the Comptroller, just now published, the following was the state of things in October, 1867, two years having then elapsed since the date of the Secretary's declaration of war upon circulating notes issued at Fort Wayne, by which the public were advised that " paper money" was too abundant, that speculation must cease, and that " contraction" must be the order of the day, the figures, as before, representing millions :—

	Banking capital.	Circulation.	Capital and circulation.	Investments.	Excess investments.
Total.	420	297	717	1103	386
New York and New England	260	173	433	677	234
All other States and Territories	160	124	284	326	152

The total circulation had, in seven years, increased 90,000,000, but instead of finding that increase in those parts of the country in which credit least abounded and circulating notes were most needed, we find the whole of it, and even 10,000,000 more, to have been distributed by the then Comptroller, and now Secretary, to those very States in which credits were most abundant and a paper circulation least required.

Comparing now the bank-created currency of the two periods, we obtain the following figures:—

	1860.	1867.	Increase.
New York and New England, present population 7,000,000—			
Credit currency	135	234	
Circulation	73	173	
Total	208	407	199
Other States and Territories, population 30,000,000—			
Credits	43	152	
Circulation	134	124	
Total	177	276	99

In the first, population could have but very slightly grown. In the other it had increased to the extent of many millions, and yet, while nearly two hundred millions had been added to the one, less than one hundred had been secured by the latter. Such has been the working of a system that is styled national, but that is not only sectional as regards the North and the South, but also as regards the Centre and the West as against the North and the East.

In the intervening period the necessities of our people for a general medium of circulation had grown south and west of New York thrice more rapidly than in the country north and east of the Delaware. In many of the older States, poorly supplied before, the check and draft currency had wholly disappeared. Throughout the West new territories had been settled, and new States had been created, in which credit had as yet obtained no foothold whatsoever. Nevertheless, in the vast region south and west of New York, with four-fifths of the total population of the Union and two-thirds of its wealth, the quantity of circulation granted by the financier who has so much complained of the "plethora of paper money" has been, as here is shown, $10,000,000 less than it had been when Kansas was but beginning to be settled, and when many of the present States and territories had scarcely yet found a place on any map whatsoever.

Bad as is this exhibit, and much as such a state of things must tend to prevent the approach of financial peace, that presented by an examination of the operations of our chief commercial cities is infinitely worse, as I propose to show in another letter, meanwhile remaining, very truly and respectfully, yours,

GEN. U. S. GRANT.   HENRY C. CAREY.

PHILADELPHIA, Dec. 25, 1868.

LETTER EIGHTH.

Dear Sir :—

Circulating notes, as the Secretary assures us, are least needed where credit currency most abounds. Cities, then, are the places at which banks least need to avail themselves of the privilege of furnishing circulation. That such was the practice under the State bank system is well known to all. How it is now, under the one organized by the Secretary himself, and how his system compares with that he had found established, is shown by the following figures, representing, as before, millions:—

OCTOBER, 1860.

	Capital.	Circulation.	Capital and circulation.	Loans.	Excess of loans.
New York	69	10	79	123	44
Boston	35	7	42	64	22
Philadelphia	12	3	15	27	12
	116	20	136	214	78

OCTOBER, 1867.

New York	75	35	110	241	131
Boston	42	24	66	101	35
Philadelphia	16	11	27	59	32
	133	70	203	401	198

Of $90,000,000 addition to the currency in that form of which the Secretary is now so generally accustomed to speak as "paper money," no less than $50,000,000 are here shown to have been given, and given, too, by himself as Comptroller of the Currency, to those three communities in which, by his present showing, circulating notes had been least required; $10,000,000 having at the same time been *withdrawn* from the country south and west of New York, embracing States and Territories almost forty in number, with a population numbering little less than 30,000,000, and growing by millions annually, the needs of these for some general medium of circulation being, man for man, thrice greater than those of the people of the cities whose past and present have been above described. The Secretary's theories, as given in the passage of his report heretofore quoted, are excellent. Can he now explain why it is that his practice has been so different?

The bank-created currency of those cities at the same periods may thus be stated:—

	1860.	1867.
Credits based on loans of moneys at the credit of individuals	80	[1]198
Circulation	20	70
	100	268

[1] This is probably much less than the truth, there being checks and "cash items" that to some extent must have borne interest. Opposed to them there are surplus funds which are additions to capital. The one would probably balance the other. 4

The Secretary denounces speculation, and professes to be earnest in his desire to put it down. Nevertheless, here, *in the very centres of speculation*, three great trading cities, we have, under a system organized by himself, an *increase* of currency amounting to $168,-000,000, or within little more than $60,000,000 of the *total* quantity that, excluding Philadelphia, is allowed to all the States and Territories of the Union south and west of New York, with four times the population and with twice the wealth of New York and New England. Not content, even, with this, the great opponent of speculation and of " paper money" has been unwearied in his efforts still further to deplete the centre, the west, and the south, and to perfect the centralization already so far established, by compelling all their banks to provide in one alone of them funds for redemption of their circulation, after having already provided for the same by deposits in his own hands at Washington. A better provision for maintenance and extension of the speculative spirit, so often and so bitterly denounced by himself, and for preventing resumption either now or at any future time, could scarcely have been devised.

The 50,000,000 additional circulation thus injected into the great centres do more, my dear sir, to cause " inflation," than would be done by 500,000,000 of the one, two, and five dollar notes required " for the retail trade, for travelling expenses, and for the purchase of products at first hands," those purposes for which the money is really, in the Secretary's view, to be regarded as a " necessity." By whom, however, were they so injected? By the Secretary himself, in his capacity of Comptroller of the Currency! He, therefore, it is, who is to be regarded as the great " inflationist;" yet does it please his friends to style as such all those who fail to see that resumption of specie payments can by any possibility be attained by means of measures tending to total destruction of the societary circulation.

" Capitals," said Mirabeau, " are necessities, but if the head is allowed to grow too large, the body becomes apoplectic, and wastes away." That, precisely, is what is here occurring, the whole tendency of the present monopoly system being in the direction of causing accumulation of blood in and about the societary heart, to the utter destruction of circulation throughout the body and limbs. Hence it is that property in New York city has attained such enormous prices, and that we are now daily called upon to read of the " unparalleled advance" that, according to the *Tribune*, chief advocate of prompt resumption as it is, has taken place in the adjoining States, New Jersey and Connecticut. Passing outward, however, south and west, we find a totally different state of things, miners, and laborers being thrown altogether idle, and the depression there being quite as little to be " paralleled" as is the advance in the States so liberally patronized by our consistent Finance Minister.

To find his system working in full perfection we need, however, to look further south—to Georgia, Carolina, and Alabama. Doing this, we find the special advocate of the Secretary's most unphilosophical and most exhaustive system, speaking to its readers in the words that follow :—

" A correspondent, writing from Hinesville, Liberty County, Georgia, says: ' A sale has taken place at this county seat that so well marked the extreme depression in the money market that I send you the particulars: Colonel Quarterman, of this county, deceased, and his executor, Judge Featter, was compelled to close the estate. The property was advertised, as required by law, and on last court day it was sold. A handsome residence at Walthourville, with ten acres attached, out-houses, and all the necessary appendages of a first-class planter's residence, was sold for $60. The purchaser was the agent of the Freedmen's Bureau. His plantation, four hundred and fifty acres of prime land, brought $150; sold to a Mr. Fraser. Sixty-six acres of other land, near Walthourville, brought three dollars; purchaser Mr. W. D. Bacon. These were all *bona fide* sales. It was court day, and a large concourse of people were present. The most of them were large property owners, but really had not five dollars in their pockets, and in consequence would not bid, as the sales were for cash.' In Montgomery, Alabama, lots on Market Street, near the Capitol, well located, 50 feet by 110 feet, averaged about $250 each. The Welsh residence on Perry Street, two-story dwelling-houses, including four lots, sold for $3500; Dr. Robert M. Williams was the purchaser. The same property in better times would not have brought less than $10,000. The Loftin Place, near Montgomery, containing 1000 acres, was recently rented at auction for forty cents an acre. The same lands rented the present year for three dollars an acre. About thirty real estate transfers were recorded in Nashville last week; prices were low. In Portsmouth, Virginia, a house and lot, formerly of the Reed estate, situated on the south side of County Street, near the intersection with Washington, was recently sold to Mr. Ames for $750. A building lot at the intersection of South and Bart Streets, brought only $125. A portion of Woodland, the late Judge John Webb Tyler's estate in Prince William County, Virginia, has been purchased by Mr. Delaware Davis, of New Jersey, at $20 an acre."

The more the blood is driven to the heart the more do the limbs become enfeebled, and the greater becomes the liability to paralysis, to be followed by death. The Secretary has been, and still is, driving all the blood of the Union into the States and cities of the north and east, and with every step in that direction the circulation becomes more and more torpid and the paralysis more complete.

§ 2. Of the agricultural departments of France a very large proportion are steadily declining in population, the main reason therefor, as given in a highly interesting paper recently published,* being to be found in " a total absence of that power to supply themselves with circulating notes which elsewhere results from the presence of banks or other establishments of credit, or that of individuals whose signatures to such notes command the public confidence."

Agriculture, for this reason, fails in those districts to obtain the aid of capital, except on conditions so onerous as to be ruinous to the borrower. Just so has it always been throughout more than half the Union; the farmers of the Mississippi Valley, and the planters of the South and Southwest having been, even before the war, compelled to pay for the use of circulating notes twice, thrice, and often even five times the rate of interest paid by their brother agriculturists of New England and New York.

So did it continue to be until the needs of war compelled the Treasury to do that which it should long before have done, furnish a national machinery of circulation, by means of which the farmer might be enabled to buy and sell for cash, and to pay in cash his mason

* Journal des Economistes, Septembre, 1867

and his carpenter; thereby, and for the first time in our history, enabling these latter in their turn to acquire that feeling of real independence which results from exercise of power to choose among contending shopkeepers that one which would most cheaply supply the cloth, the coffee, or the sugar required by their families and themselves. At once the whole position of affairs was changed; the needy farmer and laborer, begging for credit, disappearing from the stage, and the anxious trader, begging for their custom, taking their place. It was a revolution more prompt, more complete, and more beneficial than any other recorded in financial history; its effect having been that of supplying the inferior, the most useful, and the least dangerous currency—*the note*—to those portions of the country which, while abounding in labor and in natural wealth, were as yet too poor to command the services of that superior one —*the credit*—by which, in the course of time and in accordance with the Secretary's present teachings, it was to be replaced.

Of all the machinery of commerce there is none which renders so large amount of service as that which facilitates exchanges from hand to hand. The more it abounds the more rapid is the circulation, and, as in the physical body, the greater are the health, the strength, and the force. It is, however, the one that is always last obtained, and most difficult to be retained. In furnishing it gratuitously to the centre, south, and west, the Treasury rendered a larger amount of service to our whole people than it would have done had it given the gratuitous use of railroads whose *cost* would have been thrice as great as its own *amount*. That service was found in the increased demand for labor, to the great advantage of those who had it in its various forms for sale—the farmers, mechanics, and laborers of the Union. To some extent, however, it damaged those who made no profitable use of their own physical or mental faculties—annuitants, mortgagees, and other persons in the receipt of fixed incomes.

That, however, is the necessary result of beneficial changes of every kind, all such improvements manifesting themselves in an elevation of the labor of the present at the cost of accumulations of the past—the rate of interest always falling as labor becomes more productive. Instead, however, of so regarding it, those who suffered have, of course, insisted that it had been nothing but "a forced loan;" that, for that reason, it should, at the earliest possible moment, be repaid; and that the whole people should for their benefit, be deprived of all the vast advantage which, under pressure of the war, had been so promptly gained. By whom, however, had the loan been made? Had it not been by the whole body of the people? Assuredly it had, and that same body had been the recipient of its products.

It had been simply the one great corporation of the Union combining with its members for obtaining, free of charge, the use of machinery of inestimable value in default of which the societary circulation had previously been so much and so frequently arrested as to cause waste of labor to an annual amount twice greater than the circulation that had thus been furnished. It was that corporation combining with its members for their relief from the oppressive taxation of usurious capitalists, money-lenders on the one hand, and traders on the other. Of those who made the loan none complain. None suffer; there being not even a single one who cannot, on the instant, be reimbursed, obtaining from his neighbor property of value fully equal to that which he had given for his share of this, so-called "loan." What they do complain of is that, while willing to extend their loans, and to do so without charge of interest therefor, they are not permitted so to do; and here they complain with reason.

The Secretary insists, however, that this is only "paper money," of which there exists, in his opinion, so great a "plethora," that, at any sacrifice, this loan must be repaid. Seeking this "plethora," we look to the South and find plantations being almost given away, because of the almost entire absence of currency of any description whatsoever. Turning next to the Mississippi Valley we find currency so scarce that manufacturers and traders pay for its use twice and thrice the usual rate of interest; farmers, meanwhile, finding difficulty in obtaining it on any terms whatsoever.

Coming now to the centre, we find it to be so little superabundant as to compel the employment of bank certificates—a sort of bastard "paper money" that otherwise would not be used. Passing thence to the North and East, the centre of speculation, and therefore, perhaps, in both the past and the present, so largely favored by a finance minister who professes himself opposed to "speculation," we find an abundance, and perhaps even the "plethora" of which he has so much and so frequently complained. Taking, however, the whole Union, we find that of this "dishonored and dishonorable paper money" the quantity in actual circulation cannot be estimated at more than five hundred millions of dollars, or little more than a dozen dollars per head. With less than half the need of it, per head, France has a circulation more than one-half greater; and yet, with even this large supply, her agricultural districts are even now actually perishing for want of some representative of money to be employed in the effectuation of exchanges. Of all the countries of Europe there is none in which there exists in such complete abundance that superior currency which, as the Secretary assures us, and as we know to be the fact, tends to supplant the circulating note, as is the case in Britain. Yet even there we do find the circulating medium, per head, to be far greater in quantity than among ourselves. Nevertheless, with such facts before him, and in direct opposition to his own most recent teachings, the Secretary assures us that it is to the excess of "paper money" we are to look when desiring to find the "obstacle" which stands in the way of "a return to a stable currency?"

Scotland, as stated in the article above referred to, has for each 5000 of her population a place at which money operations may be transacted. Nevertheless, there is no country of Europe in which circulating notes are so generally used. This, according to the Secretary, should make of it a good place to sell in and a bad one in which to buy; there yet is none in Europe better in which both to sell and to buy.

Jersey, one of the little Channel islands, with a population of

'55,000 gathered together in a space less than half that embraced within our city limits, has no less than seventy-three places at which monetary affairs may be transacted; and yet, with all this vast machinery for supplying the superior currency, her people use of notes, none of which are of less than $5 value, more than $400,000, or almost $8 per head. Add to this the gold and silver that must necessarily be used, and we obtain a larger proportion than is now in use by a people of little less than 40,000,000, scattered over half a continent, among by far the larger portion of whom there exist none of those appliances by means of which, in more advanced communities, the use of money, whether the precious metals or the circulating note, is so much economized. Excluding New York and New England, and allowing for the general absence here of those means, the circulation of Jersey is *ten times* greater per head than that of nearly forty of our States and Territories; and yet, not only does this little island enjoy the highest degree of prosperity, but there is not a spot in Europe in which excess of currency stands less in the way of both buying and selling with advantage. The facts and the Secretary's theory do not, therefore, harmonize with each other. So much the worse, he will probably reply, for the unfortunate facts.

Such as they are, my dear sir, they are now placed before you, and none can as I think hesitate to admit the general accuracy with which they have been presented. Should your leisure permit their careful examination, you will, as I confidently believe, arrive at the same conclusion with myself, to wit: That it is to the existence of a great monopoly, created under the present banking law, we are indebted for the existence of most of those obstacles which stand in the way of a restoration of financial peace; and, that if we would remedy the evils under which we suffer, we must commence with removal of the cause to which their existence is due.

How it may be removed with permanent benefit to all, I propose to show in another letter, and meanwhile remain,

Very respectfully, yours,

Gen. U. S. Grant.   HENRY C. CAREY.
Philadelphia, December 31, 1868.

LETTER NINTH.

Dear Sir:—

Seven years since there still existed among the States in reference to one of the most important of all questions—the establishment of *institutions of credit*—a perfect equality of rights. Then, Illinois and Tennessee stood exactly on a par with New Hampshire and Vermont, and the little capitalists of Iowa found among the statutes of the Union none whose tendency was that of placing them in a position inferior to those of Maine in reference to any arrangements they might wish to make for facilitating among themselves exchanges of labor and labor's products. Among those statutes there could be found none whose direct effects had been, and must ever continue to be, that of placing the men of Missouri in the position of "hewers of wood and drawers of water" to the more favored people of New York and Massachusetts. If they still continued to barter corn for cloth, hogs for sugar, it was not because of interference of the Federal Government forbidding the adoption of measures tending towards enabling them to adopt the more civilized process of purchase and sale. If they continued to pay 20, 30, or 40 per cent. for the use of circulating notes furnished by Eastern banks, they had before them at least the hope that with time they might be enabled to establish institutions that would furnish such at more reasonable rates of interest. With the war, however, there came in this respect a total change, Congress having soon after its commencement enacted that before any association of capitalists, large or small, could be permitted to commence supplying their neighbors with machinery by means of which to make their various exchanges, they should lend to the government an amount one-ninth greater than that of the circulating notes to be supplied; and that the bonds they were thus required to buy should be placed in the Treasury, to be there held as security for payment of the notes.

That done, and the notes received, it was then further required that they should purchase a certain proportion of Treasury notes payable on demand, to be held by them as further security for payment on presentation of any portion of their own circulation. Further, in the event of failure of payment, their stockholders were made to a certain extent individually liable for any ultimate deficiency of assets, whether as regarded holders of notes, or owners of credits on their books.

Having thus defined the terms on which the several portions of the country might be allowed to obtain machinery of circulation, and *having provided such restrictions as rendered it most difficult so to do except in rich and populous districts,* it might have been supposed that then it would have been everywhere left to the people themselves to decide to what extent they would have institutions of credit empowered to supply circulating notes. Not so, however, the law providing that whensoever such circulation should have been issued to the extent of $300,000,000, all power for further issue should cease, and thus establishing a monopoly in the hands of those who first had taken possession of the little that had been allowed.

Compliance with these conditions was easy in those communities within which credit institutions already largely abounded, and in which, by the Secretary's own showing, circulating notes least were needed, to wit: New York and New England. Most difficult, however, must it prove in all of those in which such notes most were needed, to wit: the Centre, the West, and the South, those in which the superior currency of checks and drafts least existed. Most of all was it easy in those large cities in which, as the Secretary informs us, " not a fiftieth part of the business is transacted by the actual use of money;" and in which, as he further says, "except in dealings with the government, for the retail trade, for the payment of labor and taxes, for travelling expenses, the purchase of products at first hands, and for the banker's reserve, money is hardly a necessity." Such being the case, it was his duty, as Comptroller of the Currency, so to act as to secure to the States and Territories least provided with the superior currency the largest possible share of the limited quantity of the inferior one that had been thus allowed. Directly the reverse of this, however, we find him to have added $100,000,000 to the previously existing circulation of those States in which credits most existed, and $50,000,000 to that of the three cities in which circulating notes were least of all required; while actually diminishing by $10,000,000 the allowance to the whole country south and west of New England and New York.

By this course of action there was established a *monopoly of money power without a parallel in the world;* that monopoly, too, created by the Secretary himself in those very centres of speculation in which each additional million does more to produce "inflation" than could or would be done by a dozen millions scattered throughout the pockets of farmers and laborers of the east, the west, the south, or the southwest.

The counterbalance to this monopoly was found in the greenback—in machinery of circulation that had been created by the people themselves for the purpose of enabling each and all of them readily to exchange their services and products. The one tended toward giving capitalists of the cities power to compel the interior more and more to depend on them for performance of all their exchanges, and thus to give them more complete control over the farmer and the laborer. The other, on the contrary, tended toward enabling farmers and laborers to exchange among themselves freed from the control of city capitalists; and for that reason it has been that these latter, the journals in their pay, and the Treasury department, have been so unwearied in their efforts to drive it from the stage.

For accomplishment of that object they have done their utmost towards destroying the confidence of our people in each other, and in the country's future. From day to day has "contraction" been insisted on, accompanied by the assurance that prices must be made to fall; that property bought to-day must be almost valueless to-morrow; that mines opened, furnaces or houses built, this year, must prove in the next to be worth far less than cost. Raids have been made upon banks. Interest-bearing securities have been withdrawn from them for the express purpose of compelling them to heap up greenbacks in their vaults. Factories and mills have been closed that might and would have consumed hundreds of thousands of tons of coal and bales of cotton. Mines have been abandoned, and manufacturers have been ruined. Paralysis has been brought about through the whole extent of the Union, and all these things have been done to the ends that the people might be deprived of a circulating medium created by themselves and for themselves; that the monopoly of the extreme North and East might be perfected; and that the "speculator" might in this manner be driven from existence. To what extent this latter object has been attained, we may now inquire.

From the report of the Comptroller of the Currency we learn that on the first of January, 1867, the loans on private security by the banks of New England and New York were $404,000,000, and that in October following not only had there been *no contraction*, but there had been an actual *increase* of their amount.

At the first of those dates they held $297,000,000 of interest-bearing public securities. At the last, their amount had fallen $14,000,000, the whole effect of a nine months' vindictive warfare having been that of compelling them to disgorge *public* securities yielding them an annual interest of probably $800,000. Placing against this the higher interest that lenders had, by means of the Secretary's aggressive policy, been enabled to secure, the balance in favor of the banks would probably count by millions, for all of which they had been indebted to the policy announced in the celebrated but unfortunate Fort Wayne decree. The policy that carried us through the war favored those who had labor to sell and money to borrow. That of the Secretary, and of the money lenders of New York and New England, favors those who have money to lend and labor to buy; and hence it is that the societary circulation becomes daily more and more impeded, and that the Treasury daily loses power.

Throughout the North and East there was certainly a plethora of currency needing to be corrected. Has the Secretary, with all his efforts, succeeded in making this correction? On the contrary, he has not only proved himself utterly powerless in that direction, but has, by largely withdrawing that machinery on which, almost alone, were dependent the people of more than half the Union, made the centres of speculation relatively far more powerful than they had ever been before.

His policy has been wholly inoperative in all those centres of speculation in which "not a fiftieth part of the business is transacted by the actual use of money," the "plethora" still existing just where the Secretary had himself created it; monetary starvation being, meanwhile, the lot of two-thirds of the whole population of the Union, and their position, relatively to the highly speculative North and East, undergoing daily deterioration.

To what extent this course of action has tended towards facilitating resumption may be now examined.

2. The first step in that direction, whensoever it shall be made, will be the one that shall tend to replace in the Treasury the power that had been parted with at the moment when the existing monopoly had been created. As yet, every attempt in that direction has proved an entire failure, Congress having created a monster which, thus far, has proved far more powerful than its creator. Until it shall be dethroned—until it can be deprived of its present control over both people and State—there can be no financial peace, and it is with that alone that resumption can ever be brought about.

To the end that such peace may be established, we must commence by doing justice, re-establishing, under the National Banking Law, that equality of rights of which the Centre, the South, and the West so unjustly have been deprived, and thus placing the man of Missouri once again on a footing with his fellow-citizen of

Vermont. To do this must, however, as we are assured, tend
to produce inflation, to raise prices, and thus to retard resumption.
The answer to this is, that it is always expedient to do right; that
we may not do evil that good may come of it; that universal
experience teaches us that honesty is the best policy; and, that the
road towards financial peace *cannot* lie in the direction of enabling
the rich of the North and East to grow daily richer at the sacrifice
of the rights of the poorer men, white and black, of Missouri and
Minnesota, Georgia and Mississippi.

By whom, however, is it that such assertions are made? Is it
not by the people of New England, who have, with their very
limited population, secured to themselves a third of the whole
money power of the Union? Is it not by men of New York, that
other State which has secured to itself a fourth of the whole circulation allotted to more than forty States and Territories, extending
over almost an entire continent? Is it not by those cities of the
North Atlantic Coast, which have, by means of the present banking
law, secured to themselves so nearly all the power to furnish circulation which, before the war, had been exercised by interior banks?
Is it not, everywhere, by the men who desire to see a rise in the
price of that great commodity, money, of which they have the command, and a decline in the prices of those they need to purchase—
to wit, labor and labor's products? To all these questions there
can be no answer other than this: that we are in the midst of a
financial war whose object is the maintenance of a monopoly hostile
to the best interests of the people; a monopoly pending whose
existence there can be no resumption; and, *that the first step toward peace is to be found in such a re-establishment of governmental
power as would result from dissolution of the present alliance
with that portion of the community which desires that money may
be dear and labor cheap.* Throughout the war the Treasury was
in close alliance with those who desired that money might be cheap
and labor dear, and if it desires now to bring about resumption it
must commence by renewal of that understanding with the men
who have labor to sell and money to buy which was brought to an
untimely end at the moment when the Secretary, three years since,
fulminated from Fort Wayne his declaration of war upon the credit
of both the people and the State.

3. That the physical body may be sound in health, there must
be steady and rapid circulation throughout the whole system,
from the heart to the extremities, and thence back again to
the heart. So, too, it is with the social body, societary health
being entirely inconsistent with excessive circulation in the region
of the heart, the extremities meanwhile becoming from time to time
more entirely palsied, as is now the case throughout the Union.
That this may be corrected, and that there may be established or
re-established throughout the Centre, the South and the West, that
rapidity of circulation without which there can be neither financial
nor political health, we need an abolition of monopoly privileges.
That we may then gradually calm the unnatural excitement existing in States and cities which now profit of that monopoly we need
the adoption of measures tending to regulate the exercise of that

power over the currency which results from excess of loans and creation of credits on their books at one moment, and violent diminution
of loans and suppression of credits at another, the two combining
for the production of excitement at one moment and paralysis at
another, and for prevention of anything like permanent financial
peace. To that end we need a law declaring—.

First, that no bank shall hereafter so extend its investments as
to hold in any form other than those of gold, silver, U. S. notes,
or notes of national banks, more than twice its capital:

Second, that in the case of already existing banks whose investments are outside of the limits above described, any extension
thereof beyond the amount at which they stood on the first of the
present month shall be followed by instant forfeiture of its charter.

Having thus established a check upon further extension, the
next step should be in the direction of bringing the operations of
existing banks within proper limits. To that end, we need a provision imposing on all investment outside of the limits above
described a tax for the present year of one per cent. In the
second year let it be made 1½ per cent.; in the third, 2; and in the
fourth, 3. Thenceforth let the tax grow at the rate of a half per
cent. per annum until, by degrees, all banks shall have so enlarged
their capitals, or so reduced their loans, as to free themselves from
its further payment.

Holding interest-paying securities to no more than double its
capital, a bank would be always in a condition of perfect safety,
and could give to its stockholders dividends of at least 10 per cent.
Such stock would be preferable to almost any other securities in
the market, and there would be no difficulty in so enlarging the
foundation as to give to the whole structure the form of a true
pyramid, instead of that inverted one which now presents itself to
the eye of all observers.

Under the State bank system city banks furnished little or no
circulation. Why? Because their deposits enabled them to do
all the business required for making liberal dividends among their
shareholders. The country banks then monopolized the circulation. Why? Because with deposits small in amount and without the profits of circulation they could not live. Let us have
such a law as is above described and the city banks will at once
find themselves forced to relinquish to their country competitors
the whole business of furnishing circulating notes; and thus a second
great step in the direction of ultimate resumption will have at once
been made.

It may be said, however, that banks are now so heavily taxed by
both State and Federal Governments as to make it difficult under
such restrictions to continue the business in which they are now
engaged, and that it is so is probably the case. That it may so
cease to be, let the Treasury at once relinquish the few millions of
revenue which result from bank taxation, at the same time providing against increase on the part of the States. In the whole
list of taxes there are none so injurious, none which should be so
carefully avoided, as those which tend to prevent the formation of
institutions of credit; yet are State and National Governments

vying with each other in the effort so to squeeze them as almost to
drive them from existence! Were all bank taxes abolished; were
the monopoly extinguished; and were governments to encourage
rather than prevent the formation of such institutions; we should
then be on the road towards raising the greenback to a level with
the gold and silver coin. For every dollar so relinquished twenty
would.be added to the productive power of the nation as a consequence of the growth of faith in the future which.would result from
making that one step in the direction of financial peace.

4. The third step would be found in requiring banks to retain,
in lieu of the greenbacks now required, all the gold received from
the Treasury as interest on bonds therein deposited. Had this
course been pursued for three years past they would this day hold
sixty millions of gold, while the people would have in daily use an
equal amount of circulating notes that now are hoarded. Let it
be now adopted, the banking monopoly being simultaneously
abolished, and the day will then be close at hand when the amount
of interest payable to banks will reach $30,000,000 per annum;
when the world at large will see that the day is fast approaching
on which the greenback is to stand upon a par with gold and silver;
and, that if their circulation be still continued it will be because
our people will then have arrived at the conclusion that the way to
insure steadiness of monetary action is to be found in the direction
of maintaining the use of *a national medium of circulation not liable
to be withdrawn on every occasion of disturbance in the relations of
the always belligerent powers of Europe.*

5. The national banking law abounds in serious defects, all of
which must be remedied before we can have perfect financial peace.
Most important of all, however, are those above referred to, by
the one of which there was created a Procrustean Bed measured
for a body that has already, though yet in infancy, far outgrown
it; while by the other there was placed in the hands of a limited
number of persons, chiefly city bankers, a power so excessive that
it has enabled them to set at defiance all the power of the government, and will, without action such as is above described, enable
them so to do forever in the future.

By removal of the first we shall free ourselves from the absurd
position in which we at this moment stand, that of having proposed
to establish through the South a system under which money wages
were to be paid, at the same time refusing to either South or West
that power for creating the machinery in which such payments
must be made, which is so freely exercised throughout the North
and East.

By means of the second we shall not only greatly limit the power
to produce financial disturbance, but also do very much towards
limiting that extravagance of expenditure to which we stand now
indebted for an adverse balance of trade in face of which resumption can never seriously be thought of, and can, certainly, never be
brought about.

The three together furnish *the only terms* upon which financial
peace can ever permanently be secured.

That we may have political peace, and that the Union may be

maintained, we *must* begin by recognizing the existence of perfect equality among the States in reference to the power of their people to determine for themselves what shall be the character of the machinery used in making exchanges from hand to hand, and to what extent it shall be used.

In another letter I shall ask your attention, my dear sir, to some facts connected with the national debt, and meantime remain, with great respect and regard,

Yours truly,

Gen. U. S. Grant.   HENRY C. CAREY.

Philadelphia, January 4, 1869.

LETTER TENTH.

Dear Sir:—

The surrender at Appomattox, though giving us, so far as regarded operations in the field, the peace that so anxiously had been desired, brought with it reason for apprehending the reverse of peace in the commercial and financial world. For several years the country had presented to view a scene of life and activity the like of which had never anywhere before been witnessed. All who had had labor or labor's products to sell had found a ready market, and among men, too, who could at once pay over the price upon which they had agreed. For the first time farmers and laborers throughout the whole country could go cash in hand seeking their supplies among those who could sell at the lowest rate. Demand had gone ahead of supply, the economy of labor thus produced exhibiting itself in the fact that, notwithstanding the absence of a million of men in the field, the nation had found itself enabled to contribute to the wants of government in a manner so remarkable as to have amazed the outside world, while almost as much astonishing ourselves. Never before had it so well been proved that in the social as in the physical body health, strength, and life are the inseparable accompaniments of rapid circulation.

Now, however, there was threatened a serious change in the power of production as well as in the machinery of circulation. For years we had had in the field hundreds of thousands of men busily engaged in the work of consumption while adding nothing to production. Thenceforth their services were to be given to increasing the supplies of food, clothing, and machinery placed at the command of our people, and there was danger lest, in the absence of governmental purchases, the machinery of circulation might prove wholly insufficient for making the exchanges work as smoothly as they till then had done. More labor would be seeking employment, and more commodities would be in market to be exchanged against labor, and any stoppage of such exchanges must not only affect the power of the whole people to provide satisfactorily for their own wants, but also greatly impair their power for aiding the various governments, local and general, amid the difficulties in which, for the moment, they were involved. The interests of all required, therefore, that rapid circulation should continue to be maintained.

Throughout the war individuals, cities, counties, States, had volunteered their aid in a manner wholly without precedent in the annals of the world. To so great an extent had this been done that it is certainly fair to estimate the voluntary donations at $600,000,000, the half of which, or $300,000,000, still remained a charge upon our people, involving payment of interest to the annual extent of little, if any, less than $20,000,000.

The interest on this local debt was probably a full seventh of that payable on the national debt. This would seem to have been but a small proportion, yet was it really an enormous one when we reflect that the local governments had been stripped of nearly every source of revenue except the lands and houses, mills, farms, and mines, that before had been so heavily taxed for maintenance of schools, roads, poor-houses, prisons, and for other matters with whose direction they stood charged. The effect of this now exhibits itself in the fact that local taxation has become so burthensome that cases could readily be cited in which the preceding falls very little short of confiscation. The sums required for payment of interest on the various public debts being fixed quantities, it followed, of course, that every diminution in the prices of labor, or its products, tended to make the burthen more severe, while just as much ameliorating the condition of those who had interest to receive and labor or its products to purchase. In the natural course of things these latter—the men who had lent the government what it needed—were certain largely to profit; and the danger was great that those who had so freely given of their little means might largely suffer by the change. Of the two, these latter were most entitled to consideration, having given of their means and pledged their properties with no expectation whatever of remuneration. To them it was of the highest importance that the demands of the National Treasury should be limited to the smallest possible amount; that no present attempt should be made to pay the principal of the debt; that taxes should as rapidly as possible be abolished; and, generally, that the national power should be so exerted as to maintain that confidence in each other, and in the Union at large, by which the war had been so much distinguished, and to which we had been so much indebted for the success that had been obtained.

That all these things might be done; that the gap between war and peace might comfortably be bridged over; that the men who had labored and had given of their means might not be sacrificed for the benefit of those who had merely lent at heavy interest; and, that the power of the nation to contribute to the further support of government might remain unimpaired; it was essential that the Finance Minister should be capable of recognizing the truth of that proverb which teaches that those who *give* freely *more healthily, and those who more healthily have the best chance of life.* Directly the reverse of this, we have had for minister a man whose whole period of office has exhibited a series of convulsions brought about by himself and having for their effect that of making the rich richer and the poor poorer, more fully proving to the world how large is the amount of mischief that may be done by a man placed, as the present Secretary has been, in a position for the worthy filling of which he has not manifested possession of any single recommendation. Hardly had he been seated in his office before journalists known to be in his confidence gave to the world assurance that the price of gold was at once to be reduced, and that resumption was soon to be brought about. For the moment, however, public needs compelled retraction of such assertions. The Treasury was largely in debt to soldiers and contractors, all of whom would gladly have accepted notes payable on demand, and without interest, but the Secretary preferred competing with merchants and manufacturers by offering to take $600,000,000 at an extravagant rate of interest, coupled with a power to claim gold bonds at the end of three years' time. That sale accomplished, the country was next favored with a declaration of war against the circulating notes by means of which the government was then so greatly aiding the societary movement while saving nearly $60,000,000 per annum. Contraction was now to be the order of the day; prices were to be put down while taxes were to be maintained; the rich who held government bonds were to be made richer, while those who had given of their means to the support of government were to be made poorer; the banking monopoly was to be maintained, the national circulation being meantime withdrawn; and all these things were to be done that the Finance Minister might have placed at his disposal $24,000,000 a year to be applied to payment of principal and interest of the debt, which latter, as we were triumphantly assured, was to be speedily extinguished by means of a system whose obvious tendency was that of largely increasing the general rate of interest, thereby diminishing the power of our people profitably to employ their labor, or liberally to contribute to the support of government.

For the moment, Congress was led to give in its adhesion to the Secretary's measures of contraction. Very brief experience of its effects was, however, required for inducing it to limit its approval within $4,000,000 per month;

and but little more, happily, for causing it to be altogether withdrawn. So, too, has it been with regard to taxes, Congress having, in despite of his remonstrances, annihilated many of the most oppressive of them, and thus vetoed his schemes for burthening the present generation with actual payment of the entire debt.

That in the adoption of this course Congress has wisely acted will, as I think, be clear to all who shall carefully study the following facts : Taking the whole Union together, the average rate of interest paid by its taxpayers is not less than 15, if even less than 20 per cent. In New England, where institutions of credit and circulating notes abound, it is greatly less than this. In the Central States, where such institutions are more rare, and where circulating notes are much less freely supplied, it must exceed one per cent. per month. In the South, West, and Southwest, where such institutions have little or no existence, and where circulating notes are consequently scarce, it is greatly more than any of the figures I have named.* Those who pay these enormous rates of interest are the real parties liable, each in proportion to his means, for a debt of more than $000,000,000, for which the Treasury stands indorser. So long as that indorsement shall be continued, they can have the loan at 5 or 6 per cent. ; but when the indorsement is withdrawn the share of each individual enters into the general category of his debts, paying the rate of interest at which he is accustomed to have his needs supplied—the average of all being not less than thrice the rate of the public debt. Such being the case, it becomes clearly obvious that the various schemes which have been propounded in reference to early extinction of the debt are merely contrivances by means of which the rich are to be made richer at the expense of their poorer neighbors.

Adding now to this, that simultaneously with this enormous withdrawal of capital from the real producers of the land, there was to be a withdrawal of nearly the whole medium of circulation, we have before us a scheme of spoliation of the poor for the benefit of the rich the parallel of which cannot be found in the history of any commercial nation of the world.

§ 3. The Secretary's theory in reference to the currency, as has been shown, is in direct conflict with his practice ; the former most earnestly teaching that the need for circulating notes everywhere exists in the inverse ratio of the use of checks, drafts, and other machinery for economizing money of every kind ; the latter, on the contrary, furnishing notes in the direct ratio of the existence of that superior currency which, as the Secretary himself informs us, everywhere tends to supersede the note. So, as will now be shown, is it with reference to the public debt, his teachings being in the direction of maintaining inviolate the public faith, the tendency in the opposite direction of the public mind becoming, and that necessarily, more and more rapid as his policy is more fully carried out.

Seeing clearly that such is the present tendency, and correctly appreciating "the great interest and alarm excited by the doctrines recently promulgated," the Secretary has, in his Reports, devoted much space to hotness on the absolute necessity for paying the debt in gold, both principal and interest. Replying thereto, Congress might, my dear sir, with great propriety ask of him to show how far his own measures in the past had tended toward diminishing the amount of interest now to be paid ; toward lessening the present burthen of the debt ; toward increasing the general power to contribute to the revenue ; toward strengthening the hands of that loyal portion of our people to which we had been indebted for suppression of the rebellion, and to which alone the holders of our public securities can now, or in the future, look with any confidence for disposition to carry into full effect the covenants of the war. Admitting that this were done, let us now look to see what are the figures that must be given in the reply that would then be made.

---

* Even in Philadelphia an allowance of one per cent. per month fails to draw, within the first nine months of the year, more than two-thirds of the taxes on real estate. Failure throughout the year to profit of this large discount is followed by penalties, and yet the journals of the day show that more than 21,000 persons are at this moment in default. In estimating the average interest paid throughout the country, it is proper to take into consideration the great difference between the prices at which purchases of food and clothing may be made for cash, and those which must be paid by those who buy on credit.

In October, 1865, the total debt was $2,808,549,000, of which $1,162,000,000 were payable in gold. The total interest was $133,000,000, of which $67,000,000 were gold, and $66,006,000 currency. Admitting now that the character of the debt had remained unchanged, and taking the price of gold at 140, the quantity of lawful money to-day required for payment of interest on that amount of debt would not exceed $150,000,000.

In October last the debt stood at but $2,505,000,000, the gold portion of which had grown to $2,083,000,000. Three hundred millions less in quantity it now requires for interest nearly $130,000,000, being but $3,000,000 less than had been needed before reduction of the principal had been commenced. Of this the gold portion is $123,000,000, being, at 140, the equivalent of $173,000,-000 lawful money. Adding now to this the currency portion, say $7,000,000, we obtain as the total amount of lawful money this year required for satisfaction of claims for interest no less a sum than $180,000,000, being $30,000,000 more than had been needed when the debt, as stated by the Secretary himself, had been $300,000,000 greater. Adding further the interest on these $300,000,-000, we obtain $198,000,000 as the amount now payable by individuals or the State on the same amount of debt which had existed at the date of the decree which announced "contraction" as being the order of the day; and by means of which confidence, public and private, has been destroyed, and the societary movement so thoroughly paralyzed that the payment of even half of this enormous amount would be far more burthensome than would have been that of the whole on the day on which the Secretary entered on his most destructive career. In all other countries the public credit improves with diminution of the need for loans. Here, under our admirable system of finance, it seems, on the contrary, to deteriorate as the debt is more and more diminished.

The remarkable fact is thus presented, that precisely as the paralysis becomes more general—precisely as labor and all its products fall in price—precisely as lawful money becomes more valuable in the hands of those who hold it—precisely as it becomes less and less attainable by those who need to get it—precisely as taxation becomes more and more burthensome—precisely as these phenomena become more general throughout the land—the quantity of lawful money required for satisfaction of the claims of bondholders increases ; the poor being thus made poorer while the rich are being made richer, and banks, bankers, and treasury agents building palaces, while mills and mines are being closed, and working men and women deprived of power to obtain either the food or the clothing required by their families and themselves.

On an average the prices of labor and its products are at least a third less than had been the case at the date on which the Secretary announced to Congress and the people his determination to enforce "contraction." The $180,-000,000 lawful money of to-day would therefore purchase almost as much as could have then been bought with $300,000,000. As but half this latter sum, or $150,000,000, was then required, it is clear that the burthen of taxation for payment of interest has, except among the bondholders themselves, by means of the Secretary's policy been nearly doubled. Hence it is that the cry has become so general for discharge of the principal in lawful money! Hence it is that the word repudiation is now so freely used ! That it shall soon become universal all that is needed is that the Secretary be allowed by Congress to proceed in the substitution of gold bonds for greenbacks, and for all other securities that make no demand for gold, whether for principal or interest.

Were it not for his profession of desire to maintain the public faith there would be good reason for believing that, determined upon bringing about repudiation, he had arrived at the conclusion that the shortest road thereto lay in the direction of making the debt from day to day more burdensome. Certain it is that had such been his wish, he could have chosen no better course of operation than that so consistently pursued almost from the hour that he was so unfortunately placed in the direction of the national finances.

How this tends to produce the present demand for gold and bonds for exportation will be shown in another and concluding letter, and meanwhile I remain,

Yours very respectfully,

HENRY C. CAREY.

GEN. U. S. GRANT.
PHILADELPHIA, January 13, 1868.

LETTER ELEVENTH.

Dear Sir:—

1. Thus far the Secretary's measures have all looked in the direction of diminishing the machinery of circulation, diminishing the productive powers of the nation, and destroying both individual and national credit; and therefore is it that now, after nearly four years of peace, the Treasury is paying interest at a rate more than twice greater than that paid by England or by France — a rate nowhere paralleled among nations with any real claims to rank as civilized. As a consequence of this our institutions of credit invest their means in Treasury bonds where before the war they would have been applied to meeting the demands of commerce. As a further consequence, thousands of individuals have withdrawn themselves from the active pursuits of life, finding it more profitable, and freer from risk, to accept in the form of interest returns almost as large as were before obtained by those engaged in manufactures or in trade. Maintenance of the bank monopoly enables stockholders to obtain dividends varying between 12 and 25 per cent.; and thus, look where we may, we find the whole Treasury power to have been, and now to be, exerted in the direction of enriching the already rich, while depleting those who need to labor, those to whom it had been almost entirely indebted for the means by aid of which there had been successful prosecution of the war. With every step in this direction luxury increases and importations from abroad tend more and more to make demand for all the gold we mine and all the bonds we fabricate. With each there is a growth of absenteeism making demand, for expenditure in foreign countries, of more of the proceeds of the few commodities we have for export. Such is the result at which we thus far have arrived, a single presidential period employed by the Treasury in producing financial convulsions having done more towards the production of a great moneyed aristocracy, having interests wholly opposed to those of the people at large, than could have been the case had all that time been employed in civil war.

So long as almost millions of men had been employed in consuming food, clothing, and other commodities, while producing nothing, farmers, mechanics, miners, and workingmen of all descriptions, could have the use of credits, circulating notes, and all other of the machinery of circulation, at moderate rates of interest. With return of those millions to production there should have been increase of individual and national credit, enabling those who laboured to obtain the use of circulating notes at constantly diminishing cost; and yet, so far is this from being the case that the average rate thereof is now rapidly obtaining the height at which it had stood before the war, with constantly increasing necessity for return to the practice of buying and selling on credit which had then so universally existed. Why is this? Let us see!

At the date of the creation of the existing bank monopoly eleven States were out of the Union, while others were in a state so disturbed that their people were wholly unable to avail themselves of its provisions, and thus to establish among themselves institutions of credit such as, under State laws, had previously existed. Since then peace has been restored; new States and Territories have been organized, and old States have been readmitted; Pacific railroads have carried population through a country of immense extent that before had been unoccupied; and thus the field throughout which there now exists demand for institutions of credit, and for machinery of circulation, has become at the least thrice, and probably four times, greater than it then had been. To a large extent this change had occurred before the Secretary's declaration of financial war issued from Fort Wayne in 1865—that declaration to which we stand indebted for nearly all the financial trouble that has since existed.

Common sense and common honesty at that moment demanded of the Fed-

5

eral Government removal of all restrictions by means of which the people of the States and Territories south and west of the Hudson had been to so great an extent deprived of power to create for themselves institutions of credit and machinery of circulation, and so almost entirely made dependent for this latter on the extreme North and East. Had their demands been acceded to, had justice been done, and had the monopoly then been terminated, there would have arisen throughout all that vast territory a demand for Treasury bonds to be deposited in the Treasury itself as security for circulation, to the extent of at least $300,000,000, *thereby so far diminishing the necessity for sending them abroad as would have made a difference of little less than that entire sum in the price received for those that needed to be exported.* The man who *must* go to market *must* pay the cost of getting there, whether his commodity be corn, cotton, or bonds, and there is no commodity that so much as these latter is affected by any increase in the quantity forced upon the market. Every step of our finance minister tended to produce such increase, and hence it is that the position in which, so far as regards rates of interest, we at this moment stand so nearly approaches that of the least civilized portion of the European world.

While thus by destroying the domestic market doing all in his power to increase the export of bonds, nothing has been omitted that could tend to diminish their money value in the eyes of foreigners. The greater the work to be accomplished, the less, as it seemed, must be the time allotted for having it done. Hundreds of millions of bonds were forced upon the market having but three years to run. Hundreds of other millions, bearing no interest and payable only at the pleasure of the government, were forthwith to be extinguished. Hundreds of millions of three year bonds were then to be replaced by others redeemable at the pleasure of the government at the end of five years' grace. With each and every step in these directions taxes became more and more onerous and discontent more universal, and so must they continue to do until at last we shall see the people arrive, despite all honest resolutions, at final repudiation of the debt.

2. Of all maxims the greatest is that brief one which teaches that to move gently is to move safely—*festina lente.* Had the Secretary properly appreciated its value he would have desired, as far as possible, to relieve the present generation from burthens created by the war—promoting the circulation of labor and its products while postponing to a distant period payment of the debt itself, and offering the best security in his power so as to enable him most largely to reduce the rate of interest for both the people and the State. Had he so appreciated it he would have seen the great States of Europe obtaining money at low rates of interest by means of creating securities running for the longest periods, and not liable to be disturbed, and must have then been led to imitate their example. Had he so appreciated it, he would have said to Congress, that a security not liable to be paid off without consent of the holders, bearing interest at the rate of five per cent., and subject to a tax of ten per cent., could be sold far more readily than another bearing the same interest, free from tax, but liable to be paid off at the end of even thirty years.

The question of payment, whether in gold or paper, would by this process have been at once placed out of view, no holder of a bond being required to surrender it except on terms agreeable to himself.

The question of taxation of bonds, now so freely used in political warfare, would likewise have been settled.

On such terms the amount required for annual interest might have been reduced to $110,000,000, one-tenth of which would have gone to a sinking-fund by aid of which the whole debt would, before the close of half a century, have been extinguished.

Such, and better even than this, might have been the arrangement with public creditors had the Secretary sought to do even justice to them and to taxpayers as in duty he was bound to do. Directly the reverse of this, the whole period of his administration has been characterized by a determination to benefit those who had money to lend, interest and commissions to receive, at the cost of those who had taxes and interest to pay, and labor to sell. With every step in this direction there has been such an increase in the power of public creditors that it is this day thrice greater than it was four years since when the Treasury was surrounded with hungry claimants for settlement of their accounts. Then, less that two-fifths of the public debt could make demand for gold. Now, with exception of the calumniated *greenback*, nearly the whole has been so changed in form that the Treasury can make no claim for reduction of interest until it shall be prepared to offer payment in gold to all dissentients. Between bank monopolists on one hand, and bondholders on the other, it is, therefore, in a state of helplessness so pitiable as fully to account for the utter absence of faith in our financial future which now prevails, and which causes the present exorbitant demands for interest. Banks cannot be compelled to resume until the Treasury shall be pr pared to furnish gold for every greenback that may be presented for redemption. Bondholders cannot be compelled to accept low interest until the Treasury shall be enabled to offer gold in payment for the bonds already matured. In this state of things we are assured that if we will only resume, *and thereby double the already large demand for gold*, we s all be enabled to sell our bonds at lower rates of interest !

The first step towards resumption is to be found in relieving the Treasury from the double thraldom which now exists. It must be enabled to dictate law to both banks and bondholders, doing equal and exact justice to all, creditors and debtors, borrowers of money and lenders of it. To that end, the bank monopoly should be abolished, thereby creating a domestic demand for bonds. Next, we need to see the creation of a security bearing lower interest, and of such character as would enable the Treasury to say to existing bondholders that they now must choose between accepting it, *or payment.*

Such a security would be found in a six per cent. bond subject to a tax of 10 per cent., and having forty or forty-five years to run, by the end of which time, *the proceeds of the tax would have paid the debt.* Bonds deposited by banks and bankers with the Treasury might be further taxed one per cent.; and this would soon yield a further sum of five or six millions that might be so applied. Bonds thus provided for could be sold at par for gold, and the Treasury would thus be enabled to relieve itself at once from that control of public creditors which now exists, while at the same time freeing itself from all need for collecting taxes beyond the moderate sum that, as we have reason to hope, will be required for meeting current demands upon it. Thenceforward there would be peace in the financial world.

To the one who might object to this as doing too much for the public creditors the answer would be, that the loss to our whole people resulting from the paralysis produced by the present hopeless Treasury dependence counts annually by hundreds of millions ; that all arrangements thus far suggested have proved failures, and for the reason that they have involved violations of the public faith ; and finally, that every dollar thus withdrawn from the Treasury in excess of the amount demanded by even the most favorable of them would be more than tenfold made up in the increased power of production resulting from the feeling of confidence that would be produced.

At the present moment the average *public* indebtedness, of our whole population, exceeds $60 per head. Twenty years hence, to all appearance, it will not, even if undiminished, exceed $30—the power per head, to pay it having meantime more than doubled. To hesitate, under such circumstances, about making with the public creditors such fair and liberal terms as at once to command their confidence and respect would be an act of folly so great that it would be difficult to find words in which to characterize it. The more thoroughly honest a man shows himself the smaller is always the cost at which he can command the service of the capital he needs to use.

3. The Sun and the Wind had once, as Æsop tells us, a dispute as to which of them could soonest compel the traveller to lay aside his cloak, and unable otherwise to decide the question they finally concluded to bring it to a practical determination. Mr. Wind taking precedence, he blew and blew, but the louder his roar the closer became the grasp of the traveller upon his outside garment. Despairing finally of accomplishing his object, he now gave place to Mr. Sun, under the influence of whose beams the hold upon the cloak was gradually relinquished, and at length abandoned altogether.

Studying now our operations for the past three years we find Mr. Wind to have been steadily at work, treasury threats of contraction having kept nearly even pace with popular threats of repudiation ; editorial threats of forced resumption having gone hand in hand with an absenteeism which makes demand for all the gold we mine and all that we import ; increase of the public burthens travelling side by side with diminution of power for carrying the load imposed ; and the general result being that of causing every man who has anything to lose a desire to draw his cloak more closely round him, and to retire into some nook or corner of the commercial world in which he may safely stand until convinced that Mr. Wind and his companions, Clouds and Darkness, had finally abandoned the field, yielding place to the great source of light and heat, the Sun, to whom he might then look to see—

That justice be done to the people of all the States and Territories, placing them, so far as institutions of credit are concerned, and so far as law can accomplish that object, on a footing precisely the same as that now occupied by those of the Eastern States :

That justice be done to the commerce of the Union by bringing all such institutions under regulations tending to produce that regularity of action which so long has characterized the movements of those of the Eastern States:

That justice be done to such institutions wherever situated, by relieving them from taxes, and from absurd restrictions now existing, the direct effect of which is that of compelling them to overtrade and to incur risks the results of which are likely to result in ruin to their stockholders :

That justice be done to the working men who carried the country through the war, by abolishing as rapidly as possible the taxation under which so many of them now so severely suffer :

That justice be done to the public creditors, thereby securing the command of capital at the lowest rate of interest ; and finally,

That justice be done to the nation by proving to the world that in time of peace it is ready to carry into full effect the arrangements that during the war so well were understood.

With little exception the things thus proposed to be done are precisely the reverse of those which have been done since the peace, and to which we are indebted for the fact that the needs of the government for gold have been more than doubled, and, strangely enough, *as preliminary to resumption.* Let them be done, and it will soon be found that the needs, public or private, for gold will gradually decline until at length the greenback and the gold piece will stand on a level with each other, doing this as a consequence of an infusion of the superior currency of notes similar to that which now exists in Massachusetts, *the State which always pays gold, because none of her citizens need it.*

The course thus proposed would speedily extinguish the debt, doing this by means of a saving of interest consequent upon giving security of the highest order, as is always done by the great European States. Giving us peace it would inspire a confidence that would so stimulate production that taxation might soon cease to exist except in cases where its burthens are scarcely felt. Reducing the general rate of interest it would place our people more nearly on a level, in this respect, with those of Europe, and thus would largely contribute towards giving us that industrial independence without which there can be no political independence.

Sincerely hoping that such may prove to be the case, and begging you to excuse my repeated trespasses on your attention, I remain, with great regard and respect,   Yours very truly,

                                        HENRY C. CAREY.

Gen. U. S. Grant.
Philadelphia, January 13, 1869.

P. S. January 19.—The Senate Finance Committee has just now reported a bill nominally providing for resumption, but really for sacrificing all who have interest to pay, or labor to sell, at the shrine of those who have money to lend or labor to buy. Its true title would be—" An act providing for doubling the rate of interest throughout the country ; for making the rich richer and the poor poorer ; for bankrupting the people and the State ; for postponing indefinitely a return to use of the precious metals ; and for effectually securing repudiation of the national debt."

www.ingramcontent.com/pod-product-compliance
Lightning Source LLC
Chambersburg PA
CBHW030716110426

42739CB00030B/601